KARL FRENCH *on*

Bloomsbury Movie Guides

KARL FRENCH *on*

Apocalypse Now

Bloomsbury Movie Guide No.1

BLOOMSBURY

To Fiona

Published by Bloomsbury Publishing, New York and London.
Distributed to the trade by St. Martin's Press

A CIP catalogue record for this book
is available from the Library of Congress

ISBN 1-58234-014-5

First published in Great Britain 1998 by Bloomsbury Publishing Plc.

First U.S. Edition 1999
10 9 8 7 6 5 4 3 2 1

Typeset by Palimpsest Book Production Limited,
Polmont, Stirlingshire

Printed in Great Britain by
Clays Ltd, St Ives plc

Introduction

It is thirty years since John Milius wrote his first draft of the screenplay for *Apocalypse Now*, and twenty years since the film was completed. It was one of the most artistically and logistically ambitious film projects ever launched. It went $19 million dollars over its $12 million budget and was finished more than two years behind schedule. It resulted in one of the greatest films of all time, and was a personal triumph for its director, Francis Coppola, but also for all the many collaborators whose expertise, ideas, words, images and sounds helped to shape the film.

This book will not attempt to record every mention of and every reference to *Apocalypse Now* in books, music, art and other films. This would take up a book on its own. It has become an instantly recognisable brand name, so to refer to it or quote from it works as a shorthand to suggest or establish a certain sensibility, an atmosphere and attitude of craziness, drugginess and moral ambiguity. It is one of a handful of works of art as famous for the process of its creation as for its finished form. As *Schindler's List* represents for much of its younger audience their major source of information about the Holocaust, so *Apocalypse Now* will increasingly serve the same purpose for Vietnam.

This guide will offer a representative selection of these references – from the Clash to Duckman – to suggest how the film's influence and popularity have continued to grow. The film has become part of the culture embedded in popular imagination to the extent that it is impossible to hear 'The Ride of the Valkyries' without imagining Hueys on a dawn raid, or to hear '(I Can't Get No) Satisfaction' without thinking of a water-skier pulled upriver by a PBR.

The book will offer brief profiles of the film-makers and actors, explore individual scenes and characters, and try to identify their historical, cinematic, literary and mythological sources. It incorporates original interview material from William Hokanson, a Vietnam veteran, Stephen Bach, a United Artists executive at the time of *Apocalypse Now*'s production, Richard Marks, Walter Murch and John Milius. It is a product of, and investigation into, the film's enduring fascination.

A

Aardvark is Ready for War, The

The end, at least one of the chief aims, of any self-respecting alphabetically arranged guide is to begin with an entry for aardvark.

The Aardvark is Ready for War (Doubleday, 1997), a first novel by James Blinn, a US Navy veteran, is described as 'A novel of the Gulf War – a *Catch-22* of the on-line culture'. The narrator, nicknamed Aardvark (because of the appearance of a man in a gas mask), a US military surveillance expert, is given an impromptu review of the film by his colleague, Nerdy:

> *Apocalypse Now*, 1979. **Martin Sheen, Marlon Brando, Robert Duvall, Dennis Hopper. Francis Ford Coppola**'s 40 million dollar epic adaptation of **Joseph Conrad**'s novella ***Heart of Darkness***. Coppola's vision of war is manic, surreal, and overwrought in this lily white, pinko-sympathizer mockery of the manly act of halting the dreaded march of communism. Color, 153 minutes, rated R.

The novel also includes a scene in which a military plane is daubed, like **Kilgore's helicopter**, with the slogan 'Death From Above' and the throwaway line 'I love the smell of **napalm** in mosques'.

Academy Awards

Apocalypse Now received eight nominations. At the 52nd Academy Awards in 1980:

- **Vittorio Storaro** won for Best Cinematography;
- **Walter Murch**, Mark Berger, Richard Beggs and Nat Boxer won for Best **Sound**;
- in Best Film it lost to *Kramer vs. Kramer*;
- in Best Director **Coppola** lost to Robert Benton (*Kramer vs. Kramer*);
- in Best Screenplay based on material from another medium (the only official acknowledgement of **Heart of Darkness** as the film's source) **Coppola** and **John Milius** lost to Robert Benton (*Kramer vs. Kramer*);
- in Best Supporting Actor **Robert Duvall** lost to Melvyn Douglas (*Being There*);
- in Production Design **Dean Tavoularis** lost to Phil Rosenberg, Tony Walton, Edward Stewart and Gary Brink for *All That Jazz*;
- in Film **Editing**, **Richard Marks** and Walter Murch lost to Alan Heim for *All That Jazz*;
- **Martin Sheen** was nominated for Best Actor but asked for his nomination to be withdrawn.

At the previous year's awards ceremony, Francis Coppola found himself in the strange position of announcing as the winner of the Oscar for Best Film *The Deer Hunter*, a major Hollywood **Vietnam War film** (released a year before his own) directed by an Italian-American, Michael Cimino, whom Coppola greeted as 'paisan'.

acid

LSD, lysergic acid diethylamide, $C^{15}H^{15}N^2CON(C^2H^5)^2$. It was first isolated in the 1930s and on 16 Friday April 1943 the Swiss chemist Dr Albert Hofman accidentally ingested some and experienced its hallucinogenic effects with apparently no harmful side-effects. It came to prominence as an aid to psychotherapy in America in the 1950s, Cary

Grant being a noted champion of its usefulness in his own therapeutic sessions. Aldous Huxley was the foremost literary enthusiast. Timothy Leary, a Harvard therapist, was introduced to the drug in 1960 and spent much of the decade proselytising, and acted as a link between the literary acid-heads – Ken Kesey, Allen Ginsberg, William Burroughs – and those in rock 'n' roll – the Beatles, Bob Dylan, everyone on the West Coast. Acid and **marijuana** were key ingredients of the 1960s, shaping looks and sounds and attitudes, and so inevitably formed a part of the **Vietnam War** experience: a **rock 'n' roll war** with infamously young combatants. **George Lucas** has said that when they were originally developing the story 'nobody knew that there were **drugs** over there'. But **Milius**, here as elsewhere, grounded his mythical tale with authentic details and incidents.

As the boat is approaching **Do Long bridge** ('the asshole of the world'), **Chef** (**Frederic Forrest**) approaches **Lance** (**Sam Bottoms**).

CHEF: I mean what's a what's the matter with you? You're acting kind of weird.
LANCE: Hey, you know that last tab of acid I was saving?
CHEF: Yeah.
LANCE: I dropped it.
CHEF: You dropped acid. Far out.

Although Sam Bottoms has said that he and other members of the cast and crew dropped acid during the shooting, he explained that he acted the Do Long bridge scenes under the influence of speed, **marijuana** and alcohol. Lance calls the smoke he wafts around after the Do Long bridge sequence **Purple Haze**, which was originally the name of a particular brand of acid.

Acid may also conceivably have contributed to **Dennis Hopper**'s performance. While making *Easy Rider*, during the shooting of which countless joints were smoked in front of the camera, he and **Jack**

Nicholson dropped acid together on D. H. Lawrence's tomb, with Nicholson eventually coming round forty feet up a tree.

Air Cavalry

> *Choppers were what the Cav was all about.*
>
> **Michael Herr**, *Dispatches*

The **helicopter** division charged with escorting **Captain Willard**, the **boat** and its crew to the mouth of the **Nung river**. They are a troop of beer-drinking, surf dudes who fly into battle with Wagner blaring out of their helicopters, under the charismatic command of **Colonel Kilgore** (**Robert Duvall**).

As the **voice–over** narration suggests, the Air Cavalry are really the descendants of the US Cavalry, who 'cashed in their horses for choppers'. Kilgore sports a Stetson, yellow scarf and a pearl–handled revolver. **Colonel John B. Stockton**, one of the real-life models for the character of Colonel Kilgore, said, 'You wanted every member of the unit to start believing that he's in the best unit in the United States Army. We're different. We're different because we're better. And these [the insignia, the black Stetson, the spurs, etc.] are the signs, the visible signs that we're better and, if you don't believe us, just step outside the squad hut and we'll find out.'

Their eccentric, maverick behaviour is distilled from accounts **Milius** heard of his friends' experiences, and documented events from, among others, the photographer Philip Jones Griffiths. Michael Herr wrote of, 'the most comforting military insignia in all of **Vietnam**, the yellow and black shoulder patch of the Cav'. They have no obvious source in *Heart of Darkness* or any clear parallel in *The Odyssey*, but on a good day one could suggest an equivalence to the Munchkins from *The Wizard of Oz*, starting them off on their journey.

air strike

See **end, the**.

Angkor Wat

As **Eleanor Coppola** writes in *Notes* regarding the design and construction of **Kurtz**'s compound, 'They were working from **Dean**'s [**Tavoularis**] drawings and photographs of Angkor Wat.' Angkor Wat is the largest and best-preserved of the several **temples** in Angkor, a city complex of the Khmer dynasty which dominated Cambodia and much of Indo-China between the ninth and twelfth centuries AD. It provides an appropriate model for Kurtz's **jungle** compound for various reasons. It contains Buddhist carvings, which help to underpin the film's mythical and literary associations and feature in the film's symmetrical framing device. Second, it, like Kurtz's temple, conveys the impression of simultaneously springing from the heart of the jungle and being reabsorbed by it. Third, it was several times 'rediscovered' by missionaries and colonial officials, which reflects the Western, dominant arrogance of Kurtz.

Angkor Wat was used as the setting for the climax of the 1965 film of **Conrad**'s *Lord Jim*.

Apocalypse Now

Although of course the title is never mentioned in the film, it does appear fleetingly in the background as **the photo-journalist** first leads **Willard** around the edges of **Kurtz**'s compound, and we see graffiti on the **temple** stones:

OUR MOTTO

APOCALYPSE NOW

Arc Lights

As the **PBR** carrying **Willard** heads down the coast to the scheduled rendezvous with the **Air Cavalry**, Willard's reading of the dossier on **Kurtz** is interrupted by a couple of thunderous explosions:

CHEF: What's that?
WILLARD: Arc Light . . . B-52 strike . . .

CLEAN: Concussion'll suck the air out of your damn lungs.

In *A Bright Shining Lie*, Neil Sheehan writes:

> The B–52s of the Strategic Air Command, which struck under the code name Arc Light, were restricted to bombing suspected Communist bases in relatively uninhabited sections, because their potency approached that of a tactical nuclear weapon. The eight-engine jets had been converted into monster flying bomb platforms, each capable of lofting in excess of twenty tons. A formation of six B–52s, dropping their bombs from 30,000 feet, could 'take out', in the language of the airmen, almost everything within a 'box' approximately five-eighths of a mile wide by about two miles long. . . . Whenever Arc Light struck in the predawn anywhere in the vicinity of **Saigon**, the city woke from the tremor.

Clean's comment is a near quotation from Philip Jones Griffiths's description of **napalm** attacks in *Vietnam Inc.*:

> Few napalm victims are seen in the hospitals of South **Vietnam**. Because napalm is such an effective weapon, there are rarely any survivors. Even those who hide underground (the standard procedure when one's village is being attacked) are asphyxiated because the fire storm causes a vacuum above ground. As every GI knows, 'it just sucks the air outta their lungs'.

Archangel

'Operation Archangel' was the code-name for the unsanctioned (and in the film unspecified) operation in October 1967 for which **Kurtz** as a 38-year-old novice **Green Beret** was going to be officially punished until the press got hold of it. In the wake of the publicity he was promoted to colonel.

See **bullshit**.

arrows

This strange attack survives almost unchanged in the translation of *Heart of Darkness* into *Apocalypse Now*. In the novella the boat carrying **Marlow** heads upstream towards **Kurtz**:

> Then I had to look at the river mighty quick because there was a snag in the fairway. Sticks, little sticks, were flying about, thick; they were whizzing before my nose, dropping below me, striking behind me against my pilot-house. All this time the river, the shore, the woods were very quiet – perfectly quiet. I could only hear the heavy splashing thump of the stern-wheel and the patter of these things. We cleared the snag clumsily. Arrows, by Jove! We were being shot at! I stepped in quickly to close the shutter on the land-side. That fool helmsman, his hands on the spokes, was lifting his knees high, stamping his feet, champing his mouth, like a reined-in horse. Confound him! And we were staggering within ten feet of the bank. . . . The twigs shook, swayed and rustled, the arrows flew out of them, and then the shutter came to. 'Steer her straight,' I said to the helmsman. He held his head rigid, face forward, but his eyes rolled, he kept on lifting and setting down his feet gently, his mouth foamed a little. 'Keep quiet!' I said in a fury.

This sequence in the film retains its links to its source through the death of **Chief** and up to his **water burial**. **Coppola**, as shown in the documentary *Hearts of Darkness: A Filmmaker's Apocalypse*, helped in the strange action behind the camera by joining in throwing the sticks on to the boat. In both film and book, this attack is later explained by the harlequin Russian trader/**photo-journalist** as a harmlessly intended last effort by Kurtz and his men to scare the boat's crew away.

assassin

As **Willard** embarks on his mission, he wonders, 'How many men had I already killed? There were those six that I knew about for sure. Close enough to blow their last breath in my face.'

Later, in **Kurtz**'s compound, there is the following exchange:

KURTZ: Are you an assassin?
WILLARD: I'm a soldier.
KURTZ: You're neither. You're an errand boy sent by a grocery clerk to collect a bill.

This is, of course, the major change in the character of **Marlow**/Willard in the transference from book to film. Willard is engaged not to bring Kurtz back but to terminate his command, to 'terminate the Colonel'. They – Willard and Kurtz – are parallel characters, both explicitly killers, but, while Willard operates with the covert support of the Corporation, Kurtz is out there 'beyond the pale of decent restraint'. Both are aware of the hypocrisy. Willard says that accusing a man of murder in **Vietnam** is 'like handing out speeding tickets at the Indy 500', while Kurtz asks, 'What do you call it when assassins accuse the assassin?'

awards

Apart from **Cannes** and the Oscars, **Coppola** won a Bafta award for Best Director, **Robert Duvall** won a Bafta for for Best Supporting Actor and *Apocalypse Now* won three awards for sound at the Golden Globes.

B

Bahr, Fax

Co-director of *Hearts of Darkness: A Filmmaker's Apocalypse*.

balls

When the **PBR** crew and **Willard** join the **Air Cavalry** on the dawn raid to secure the village at the mouth of the **Nung river**, **Chef** asks one of the men why they all sit on their helmets. The soldier shouts, 'So we don't get our balls blown off.' This supplies further evidence for Elaine Zablotny, in her piece 'American Insanity – Apocalypse Now' *Film/Psychology Review*, that the film is essentially an extended castration myth:

> In **Coppola**'s vision the central fact in the American psychosis is the feeling of castration. Images of castration appear subliminally at first, then explicitly, and then symbolically with ever more horrible variations. . . . [After Willard has punched the mirror in his **Saigon** hotel room] His face is now a grimace of extreme pain; the sheets are smeared with blood and he wads them around his genitals and collapses on the floor.

Then, in **Nha Trang**, of the recording in which **Kurtz** recalls his nightmare of the **snail** crawling along the edge of a straight razor, she argues:

> The image is kinaesthetic, reaching the viscera before the mind, for the vulnerable, mucousy body of the snail is like the lubricated genital organ.

Then she discusses this sequence on **the Huey**, the significance of Chef's **head** being dropped into Willard's lap and that of the tiny, severed arms.

The truth is probably a little more prosaic, adding another layer of authentic detail, reflecting a very real worry among soldiers. In *Dispatches*, **Michael Herr** writes of this:

> Some feared head wounds, some dreaded chest wounds or stomach wounds, everyone feared the wound of wounds, the Wound. Guys would pray and pray – Just you and me, God. Right? – offer anything, if only they could be spared that: Take my legs, take my hands, take my eyes, take my fucking *life*, You Bastard, but please, please, please, don't take *those*. Whenever a shell landed in a group, everyone forgot about the next rounds and skipped back to rip their pants away, to check, laughing hysterically with relief even though their legs might be shattered, their kneecaps torn away, kept upright by their relief and shock, gratitude and adrenalin.

Banner, Fiona

Artist who specialises in wordscapes, canvases filled with descriptions of entire films, including all the dialogue. Her exhibition *The Nam*, her rendition of *Apocalypse Now* and *Born on the Fourth of July*, has been reproduced in book form.

'Battle for Khe Sanh, The'

Article by **Michael Herr** in *Esquire* in 1968 that was the partial inspiration for **John Milius**'s original 1969 screenplay. It was a piece that Herr reworked to form the central section of *Dispatches*. Herr found himself in the midst of a virtual siege that threatened to turn into a re-enactment of Dien Bien Phu, a disastrous and decisive defeat for the French in the first Indo-China War in 1954. In fact the similarity between the two military encounters was widely noted and General Westmoreland described Khe Sanh as the North Vietnamese's 'vain attempt to restage Dien Bien Phu'. The article's influence on the film is particularly evident in the **Do Long bridge** scene.

Beach, The

Novel by Alex Garland which establishes its authentically dark, Southeast Asian credentials by including in the short prologue unattributed images that would be instantly evocative to its readers:

> Dropping **acid** on the Mekong Delta, smoking grass through a rifle barrel, flying on a **helicopter** with opera blasting out of loudspeakers, tracer-fire and paddy-field scenery, the smell of **napalm** in the morning.

beginning, the

How do you begin a film? How do you begin this film? Why not with a montage scene that contains a précis of all that is to come? That suggests the workings of the central character's mind? That depicts the cinematically beautiful effects of war and destruction? All played out against **'The End'** by **the Doors**. This choice of **music** has become a familiar joke, a pun, but it plays with the title. We begin with **the end**; the apocalypse is now; the fat hippie announces the end and will go on to sing about killing his father. This is going to be a strange trip.

Supervising editor **Richard Marks** remembers:

We were never satisfied with the early version of the film's opening. All the elements are there in the draft screenplay, but it is prosaic. You have a soldier, a CIA operative, desperate to get back into the field because he can't cope with his own life. We see him drunk, frustrated, hung-over, desperate to get back into the **jungle**, and he goes off to get his mission. You're asking the audience to identify with a hired killer and follow him on his journey up the river. But they wouldn't identify with him unless you could see his pain, by the overlay of images and his **voice-over**. As we started to cut the film, we saw that we needed an opening that contained a series of nightmarish images and emotions, that foreshadowed the experience of the film and its end.

Sound designer and co-editor **Walter Murch** also recalls how the beginning was

something that began to emerge during the shooting, and the first component of that was a shot filmed during the attack on the village, when **Kilgore** orders the big **napalm** drop so he can surf. This was a huge explosion of gasoline, and whenever you do something like that you can only do it once so you cover it with as many cameras as possible. [The napalm explosion is shown from three different camera positions in the finished film.] So they did that and one of them was a tele-photo camera that was shooting at something like 256 frames per second – a high-speed camera. During dailies, **Francis [Coppola]** looked at all these different camera positions and then along came this slow-motion tele-photo shot and Francis immediately saw the beginning of the film.

There was something about that, the green jungle, flattened by the tele-photo lens, looking very calm and peaceful and then having it suddenly erupt in red fire. It was something that, for Francis, had to do with what the whole **Vietnam** experience was about. It encapsulated what had happened in Vietnam.

So he wanted to begin the film with that and then in parallel they had shot some character improvisation with **Martin Sheen**. Because the film had already started shooting with **Harvey Keitel** playing **Willard** for a month, Martin Sheen came onto the project while it was in progress. So Francis wanted to get him up to speed as soon as possible with what the Willard character was about. They did an improvisation which they then decided to shoot with two cameras at ninety degrees to each other just to document it. Willard was on a bender in his hotel room, and it turned out that Martin Sheen at that time had an alcohol problem himself, so that merged nicely – and the alcohol he's drinking in the scene is real and he's really drunk.

He's going into his own private hell which is merging with the private hell of Willard. Also it's an attempt on everyone's part to fuse the two psychological characters together. When they were looking at it, nobody knew what was going to happen, but when they looked at it in dailies, they saw that it was really remarkable. The whole thing of smashing the mirror is something that Martin Sheen did spontaneously – nobody expected him to do it – and that blood is real blood. All of that is really happening. It was so hair-raising that they just got the idea of putting these two elements together.

Beverly Hills

The name of the bunker at the **Do Long bridge**.

See **Canned Heat**.

Bible, the

One of the books pointedly shown to be in **Kurtz's library**. It supplies the film's title, largely as an anti-flower power, pro-war joke by **John Milius**. It suggests that the dark prophesies of Revelations are being visited upon the earth both in the **Vietnam War** and in microcosm in **Kurtz**'s dark domain.

Big Wednesday

Major cult samurai-surfer-**Vietnam War Film**. **John Milius** explains:

> After *The Wind and the Lion*, I saw that *Apocalypse Now* was about to get made, I realised that I was starting to distance myself from **surfing** at that point. I'd grown up as a full-on surfer, immersed in the world of surfing. I saw that this world was disappearing, and I thought that if I don't write this soon, I'll be too distanced from it. I'd always intended to write the great surfing novel, mixing up surfing with Arthurian legends. I'd always been influenced by Ken Kesey, so I wanted to apply his style to the surfing world.

The film has the unmistakeable stamp of John Milius, blending mysticism and machismo. He wrote and directed this semi-neglected classic, which follows a group of young surfer dudes as they grow up (come of age, in film-speak) surf, go to **Vietnam** or avoid the draft, before meeting up once more to ride the awesome eponymous wave. The film's key character is the mystical board-maker who crafts a board so excellent that it can be ridden only once. One of the best films of the 1970s – see it and be stoked.

Blank, Les

Camera operator on *Hearts of Darkness: A Filmmaker's Apocalypse*, and director of the similar and similarly excellent *Burden of Dreams*, the documentary film about the making of Werner Herzog's *Fitzcarraldo*. There are several striking parallels between the two feature films and the two documentaries. Herzog and **Francis Coppola** were friends. Both documentaries show a director driven to distraction in the **jungle** while making a film based partly on fact (which involved a central part being recast after shooting had begun) and in which a hubristic Westerner treats locals like slaves and the central character undertakes a crazed boat journey through a hostile country.

Bottoms, Sam (b. 1955)

Actor born in Santa Barbara, California. He has two elder acting brothers, Joseph and Timothy, and memorably appeared with Timothy in *The Last Picture Show*. The highlight of his career so far has been playing Gunner's Mate 3rd Class, star surfer **Lance B. Johnson**, no stranger to narcotics. He appeared alongside Clint Eastwood in *The Outlaw Josie Wales* and *Bronco Billy*, and in **Coppola**'s *Gardens of Stone*. His more recent credits include the kick-boxing movie *Ragin' Cajun* and *Snide and Prejudice*.

Brando, Marlon (b. 1924)

Stage and screen actor born in Omaha, Nebraska. When looking at, or rather talking about, films you have seen so many times that they seem as familiar as (or more familiar than) incidents in your own life, you can start to play games with them the way you toy with elements of your own life. What if things had been different? I can and do defend almost every element, performance and scene in the release version of *Apocalypse Now*. But this defence becomes weakest (and most essential) for the film's **end**.

The film took a long time to make it to cinemas. It emerged organically, and as the result of a lot of good and bad luck, and meticulous planning. But it could, like many other great films – e.g. a *Casablanca* starring Ronald Reagan and Ann Sheridan – have been totally different. It could have been a low-budget black and white, 16mm, documentary-style film, shot on location in **Vietnam** or the Sacramento delta, directed by **George Lucas**, with no stars and released in 1972 to an indifferent public. What if **Harvey Keitel** hadn't got fired? What if **Jack Nicholson** had played **Kurtz**? Was Marlon Brando born to play Kurtz? Yes, in the context of the film: by his own admission, he came closer to losing himself in this role than in any other.

Brando established himself in the early 1950s as a new kind of film star (along with his peers James Dean and Montgomery Clift) of intensity, realism and ambiguous sexuality. His performance in *A Streetcar Named Desire* is a blend of barely restrained violence and camp. But his choices of projects in the 1960s were marked by bravery and eclecticism more than shrewdness. His fortunes had sunk to such a level that **Coppola** had to fight for his casting of Brando in the pivotal role of Don Corleone in *The Godfather*. This and the shocking bleakness of *Last Tango in Paris* re-established him as a major international star, who demanded and got $3.5 million for four weeks' work on location. It has been suggested that after the deposit payment of the first $1 million the fee was renegotiated in Brando's favour. This apparently meant that the actor would receive 11.3 per cent of the film's adjusted gross, and if this passed $8.8 million (which it did by approximately $100 million) he stood to make 34 cents on every ticket sold.

It was the enormity of Brando's fee, the many problems of the elongated shoot – suggesting a chaotic project and the imminent and much anticipated fall of the boy wonder Coppola – that created a storm of what was perceived as negative pre-publicity. Somehow, by chance or design, this mass of information turned the film into a major 'event' movie. In an act of calculated provocation, Coppola used the press conference at the official screening of his film at the **Cannes Film Festival** to attack the press. As Steven Bach recalls in *Final Cut*:

> He told them the press had spent four years indulging in irresponsible and malicious gossipmongering over production problems as taxing as any director had ever faced before. He told them they knew nothing about moviemaking anyway, which may have explained their irresponsibility, their gloating, their cannibalising of misinformation from each other ever since he began his movie. He told them their opinions were of little or no value, based as they were on ignorance without the mitigating grace of innocence, that whatever slings and arrows they were now preparing to hurl at his weary but indomitable frame would have no effect, because he rejected them, their opinions, their very function. Only one thing mattered, only one thing would remain, his movie, the objective quality of which he expected them neither to praise nor to perceive, and it mattered not at all that his entire future, personal and professional, was riding on it. . . . They loved it.

Elsewhere, Steven Bach explains that it was during the post-production period of his film that Coppola began to immerse himself in the world of marketing, and he came to see that Brando, and his belated appearance in the story, was the central factor in selling the film.

As is well known, Brando arrived on set not having read *Heart of Darkness*. But even if he had, what clues could it have given him, apart from the obvious disparity between the wraith-like Kurtz of **Conrad** and his own weight of over 250 lbs? As hastily conceived by Brando, Coppola and, crucially, **Storaro** (it is essential that Brando exist always only partly in the light), and with the use of a very tall stand-in, Kurtz's motivations have been crystallised, his apocalypse coming in reaction to his own side's hypocrisy and ineffectuality, and the pure, decisive will of the enemy.

Seldom can a leading character's role and speeches have been distilled to such a small size from so much in the lengthy improvisations he performed to camera. There could, I think, be still less. On a conservative estimate, I have seen the film forty times, and the ending has seemed wholly satisfactory in perhaps half a dozen of these viewings. It looks wonderful, is crammed with the suggestions of literary and mythical significance (which requires the inclusion of Brando reading the beginning of *The Hollow Men*), and much of it makes narrative sense. But Brando himself? The **gardenias** speech, presumably plucked from Brando's own memory (mixed with an inspiration from **John Milius**) is fine, establishing Kurtz's finer aesthetic tastes and qualities. The **polio** vaccination speech is powerful, and based on the experiences of the military adviser, and John Milius's friend, **Fred Rexer**. These could be Kurtz.

But the rest could be shaved down further. Brando is intelligent but, as his autobiography shows, not brilliant. As an actor he is often inspired and passionate, but he is a dilettante. Here, his Kurtz looks as if he is somehow dying (though not of starvation), and ought to be focused but suffers from mind-wandering. His mad improvisations too often sound like mad improvisations. Brando simply isn't someone whose ideas on freedom and moral **terror** you want to hear. He is a versatile actor, not a universal genius.

Still, the dénouement caused similar problems for Conrad. At the end of a thrilling nightmare journey you need an actor of extraordinary presence to embody pure genius and pure evil. No one could do this adequately but, despite the shortcomings of the film's climax, you can imagine no one coming closer to pulling off this impossible feat than Brando.

Bubba

See **Clean, Mr Clean**.

bullshit

When reading the file on **Kurtz** regarding the army's hypocritical response to Kurtz's maverick 'Operation **Archangel**', **Willard** comments, 'Oh, man. The bullshit piled up so fast in **Vietnam** you needed wings to stay above it.' This is an observation and a little play on the **Green Berets**' insignia, as depicted in the not very subtle theme song to John Wayne's rabble-rousing, red–baiting *The Green Berets*:

> Silver wings upon their chest,
> These are men, America's best.

C

camouflage

The use of camouflage is the film's gauge of the degree of the characters' absorption into the **jungle** and confrontation with darkness. It is worn by **Lance**, **Colby**, **Kurtz** and, finally, **Willard**.

Camp, Colleen

Camp plays one of the **Playboy Bunnies** in the United Services Overseas sequence. She was a sometime companion of **Coppola**.

Canned Heat

American heavy rock band of the 1960s and early 1970s, famous for 'On The Road Again', among others. They supply the nickname of the gun on board the boat under **Clean**'s control – 'Gods Country'. This – along with the 'Death from Above' on **Kilgore**'s **helicopter** and the naming of the bunker in the **Do Long bridge** scene '**Beverly Hills**' – is typical of the black humour in the rechristening of places, vehicles and **weapons**. This tendency is well illustrated in *Dispatches*, where **Michael Herr** writes of flak jackets daubed with their *noms de guerre*, fantasies (BORN TO LOSE, BORN TO RAISE HELL, BORN TO DIE) and mottoes (*YEA, THOUGH I WALK THROUGH THE VALLEY OF THE SHADOW OF DEATH I SHALL FEAR NO EVIL, BECAUSE I'M THE MEANEST MOTHERFUCKER IN THE VALLEY and EAT THE APPLE, FUCK THE CORPS*), and helmets frequently seen with the graffito *WHY ME?*

Cannes Film Festival

Coppola arrived at the thirty-second Cannes Film Festival in 1979 with a rough cut of *Apocalypse Now*. He rented a yacht in the bay for the duration of the festival. After the morning press screening at the Palais du Festival, he announced:

> My film is not a movie.
> My film is not about **Vietnam**.
> It *is* Vietnam.
> It's what it was really like.
> It was crazy . . . and the way we made it was very much like the way the Americans were in Vietnam. We were in the jungle, we had access to too much money, too much equipment, and little by little we went insane.

Apocalypse Now and *The Mission* (which itself won the *Palme d'Or* in 1986) are the only films to have been entered into competition as works in progress. The screening, described by Stephen Bach as 'the most public sneak preview in the history of motion pictures', was an enormous success. In their history of the Cannes Film Festival, *Hollywood on the Riviera*, Cari Beauchamp and Henri Béhar describe the 'overwhelmingly positive response' and remark that from 'the opening moments, with the shot of the whirling fan, the audience was enraptured'.

The jury, headed by novelist Françoise Sagan and otherwise comprising actress Susannah York, screenwriter Sergio Amidei, Rodolphe M. Arland, director Luis Berlanga, critic and film historian Maurice Bessy, Paulo Claudon, director Jules Dassin, director Zsolt Kezdi Kovacs and Robert Rodzhdestvensky, awarded the *Palme d'Or* jointly to *Apocalypse Now* and Volker Schlöndorff's *The Tin Drum*.

caretaker

As he is delivered by **helicopter** to his meeting in **Nha Trang**, **Willard** comments in his **voice-over**:

> It was no accident that I became the caretaker of Colonel Walter E. **Kurtz**'s memory any more than being back in **Saigon** was an accident. There is no way of telling his story without telling my own and if his story is really a confession then so is mine.

This is one of the closer parallels between *Apocalypse Now* and its partial inspiration ***Heart of Darkness***. **Michael Herr**, the author of this voice-over narration, clearly went back to the novella's source as this passage echoes **Conrad**'s:

> I had full information about all these things, and, besides, as it turned out, I was to have the care of his memory.

Willard fulfils this role literally, emerging from Kurtz's compound carrying his memoirs.

carabao

The animal whose sacrificial slaughter is intercut with that of **Kurtz** is referred to by **Eleanor** and **Francis Coppola** as a caribou but elsewhere as a more generic ox. Partly a serendipitous happening that occurred on location and was re-enacted for the cameras, the juxtaposition enhances the drama, the ceremonial aspect of Kurtz's death, and also presumably echoes the bizarre scene at the end of the battle which marks **Willard**'s introduction to **Kilgore**. This aerial cow sequence demonstrates the strength of the modern **Huey** helicopter and its ability to transport troops, boats, cows, whatever. It must also serve as a variant on the old Chekhov rule: if you see a cow being airlifted in Act II you can be sure that it will be slaughtered in a bizarre fertility ritual in Act V.

See **relocation**; **sacrifice**.

Carpenter, Linda

Playboy Bunny in the United Services Overseas sequence, fulfilling identical role to **Colleen Camp**.

Charlie

Charlie was the most commonly used nickname among American soldiers for the **Viet Cong**. It derives from the radio call sign for VC, Victor Charlie.

'Charlie don't surf'

Kilgore, the ultimate mad officer, here as elsewhere expresses his contempt for the **Viet Cong**. He is twice informed that the place which **Willard** and Phillips want to be escorted to is 'Charlie's point'. But he has made the instant and unshakeable decision to capture the point in a spectacular dawn raid because 'Charlie don't surf'. It seems a throwaway punch-line, which on first viewing apparently emphasises the randomness of Kilgore's motivation, but makes increasing sense on further viewings. It has become a cult line – it has a life of its own beyond the film.

Among other usages, it inspired the Clash's anti-imperialist song of the same name. The song opens and closes with an effective musical evocation of *Apocalypse Now*'s thup thup thup **quintuphonic**

helicopter beginning. It's the bits in between that are less inspired, the chorus being:

> Charlie don't surf and we think he should.
> Charlie don't surf and you know it ain't no good.
> Charlie don't surf for his hamburger mama.
> Charlie's gonna be a **napalm** star.

It has also appeared on a T-shirt of dubious significance as a slogan under a photograph of **Charles Manson**. What exactly does it mean? Is it a simple juxtaposition of two icons of the dark side of late 1960s American life, simultaneously embracing and rejecting the ethos of the **acid**/love generation? Does it suggest that **surfing** is too frivolous a pastime for a man whose vocation is to be an unhinged murderous psychotic? It is probably just a play on the name **Charlie**, and part of the misguided celebration of Manson's achievements.

Within the film the phrase symbolises the bizarre presence and twisted logic of the Americans in **Vietnam**. Kilgore is a maverick. He is looking for good surfing as much as anything else in the war. Willard tells him of the orders for the **Air Cavalry** to escort him and the boat to the mouth of the **Nung river**, but he is unmoved: 'I've been trying to forget about you.' But then one of his soldiers and fellow surfers tells him that there is a fantastic peak there: 'It's tube city.' This is the immediate clincher. As is discussed elsewhere, the Americans never really knew how to conduct the war in Vietnam. The rules of engagement for the Americans and the Viet Cong were wholly at odds – they were politically, culturally and militarily different, as is emphasised by this line.

Chef

Member of patrol boat crew played by **Frederic Forrest**. As **Willard** says in his **voice-over**, 'The machinist, the one they called "Chef", was from New Orleans. He was wrapped too tight for **Vietnam**, probably wrapped too tight for New Orleans.' This, written by **Michael Herr**, could have come straight out of *Dispatches*; in fact it reverses the image of the Lurp (long range–recon patroller), who describes the reaction to his warped behaviour when back in America on leave – aiming his hunting rifle at passers-by. '"It used to put my folks real uptight," he said. But he put people uptight here too, even.' Again in *Dispatches*, there is an exchange in the besieged Khe Sanh:

'Fuck the lieutenant,' Mayhew said. 'You remember from before he ain't wrapped too tight.'
     'Well, he wrapped tight enough to tear *you* a new asshole.'

Chef, like the other members of the patrol boat's crew (and **Kilgore**, the Corporation men, etc.) is representative of a type of American in Vietnam. He couldn't resist the draft. As with **Lance** and **Clean**, it is made clear (explicit in the voice-over) that he simply shouldn't be there. This is presumably not some subversive anti-war sentiment – there seems to be a perpetual balance in the film between the war-loving influence of **John Milius** and the more anti-war, liberal stance which provides the film's unsettling apparent moral ambiguity – but rather the reflection of the reality of the average draftee, transported from normal American life to a distant country, alien culture and incomprehensible war.

We see the whole film through Willard's eyes, but he remains impassive, while the **Chief** is busy with his boat, his orders, his anger at Willard, Clean is a bit out of it, a kid getting a buzz, and Lance is increasingly zonked. So that leaves Chef to react normally and rationally (with degrees of hysteria, fear and disbelief) on the audience's behalf to everything that happens. His background is clarified when he and Willard get out of the boat (never do that!) and walk through the eerie **jungle**, over the roots of the tree in search of mangoes:

WILLARD: Chef?

CHEF: Yes, sir.

WILLARD: How come they call you that?

CHEF: Call me what, sir?

WILLARD: Chef. Cause you like mangoes and stuff?

CHEF: No, sir, I'm a real chef. I'm a **saucier**.

WILLARD: Saucier?

CHEF: Yes, sir. Y'see I come from New Orleans. I was raised to be a saucier. A great saucier.

WILLARD: What's a saucier?

CHEF: I specialise in sauces. Then I was supposed to go to Paris, to study at the **Escoffier** school. Then I got, er, orders for my physical. Hell, I joined the Navy. Heard they had better food. Cook's school. That did it.

He goes on to describe a scene of such bad food handling that it led him to abandon the kitchen and become a machinist. This scene is clearly there to confirm him as a man as badly out of place as Donald Pleasance's ornithologist/cartographer in *The Great Escape*. There also seems to be some sly, jokey reference. In 1911, aged 19, **Ho Chi Minh**, who would eventually lead the struggle for Vietnamese unification and independence, left Vietnam for a self-imposed exile of thirty years. As Stanley Karnow explains in his excellent *Vietnam: A History*:

> After almost a year in the United States [in 1914], he sailed to London, where he found a job in the kitchen of the elegant Carlton Hotel, whose renowned chef, Georges Auguste Escoffier, promoted him to assistant pastry cook.

It seems doubtful whether there is any great significance in this gastronomic link. It could possibly act as some subliminal, subtextual message to establish a spiritual kinship between Chef, an ordinary

American, and Ho Chi Minh, the figurehead of the Vietnamese people. After all, Ho Chi Minh was not a knee-jerk Americanophobe. In fact he incorporated some of the American Declaration of Independence into his own Declaration of Vietnamese Independence in 1945. Then again, it could just be a coincidence. Chef fails to maintain a relationship with his **head**.

See **tiger**; **'Never get out of the boat'**; **decapitation**.

Chief

Phillips, captain of the patrol boat, played by **Albert Hall**. **Willard** says: 'It might have been my mission but it sure as shit was the Captain's boat.' His role has shifted somewhat from that of his equivalent in *Heart of Darkness*. There he is merely a helmsman, who meets the same fate and has the same burial. In both book and film, the character's death is there partly to stress the focus of **Marlow**/Willard on **Kurtz**, on meeting him and speaking (or rather listening) to him. In *Heart of Darkness*, after the helmsman's death Marlow tosses his own bloody shoes in the river before going on for several pages about Kurtz's greatness, eloquence and magnetic appeal. Suddenly – and rather unconvincingly, considering that the character has barely been mentioned before being dispatched – Marlow says:

> 'I missed my late helmsman awfully – I missed him while his body was still lying in the pilot-house. Perhaps you will think it passing strange for a savage who was no more account than a grain of sand in a black Sahara.'

At least he expresses some regret. The film is more extreme. The presentation of this passage may be similar in feel, but Willard has become rather taciturn (except in the **voice-over**). Insanely driven and single-minded, he is a figure of near-pure will who must meet

Kurtz to become complete. The half-hearted concern and brief mourning from the novel is transferred in the film to Chief himself, who embraces the dead **Clean**. The burial of Chief is performed by **Lance**.

Although he isn't fully fleshed out, Phillips is at least a real character. He is one of the film's few 'sane' figures, representative of the disproportionate number of black soldiers in **Vietnam**, and he is crucial to the progress of the film and journey. Early on in the story he delivers a short key speech to emphasise for us and Willard that they and we are heading for a very bad place. As they are moving along towards their meeting with the **Air Cavalry**, he tells Willard:

> You know I pulled a few special ops in here. About six months ago I took a man who was going up past the bridge at **Do Long**. He was regular army too. I heard he shot himself in the head.

This is a beautifully concise anecdote, clearly inspired by the exchange between Marlow and the Swedish steamer captain as they head up the coast to the mouth of the big river in *Heart of Darkness*:

> 'As we left the miserable little wharf, he tossed his head con-temptuously at the shore. "Been living there?" he asked. I said, "Yes." "Fine lot those government chaps – are they not?" he went on, speaking English with great precision and considerable bitterness. "It is funny what people will do for a few francs a month. I wonder what becomes of that kind when it goes up country?" I said to him that I expected to see that soon. "So-o-o!" he exclaimed. He shuffled athwart, keeping one eye ahead vigilantly. "Don't be too sure," he continued. "The other day I took up a man who hanged himself on the road. He was a Swede, too." "Hanged himself! Why, in God's name?" I cried. He kept on looking out watchfully. "Who knows? The sun too much for him, or the country perhaps."'

The Chief doesn't waste words and we are left in no doubt that this mission, the film, has the perverse counter-intuitive logic and structure of a horror film, with the characters wilfully travelling in the wrong direction – towards not merely danger but what is explicitly 'the worst place in the world'.

The Chief 'don't smoke', and with good reason – possibly even intuition – hates and mistrusts Willard.

See **water burial**; **racism**; **spear**.

Citizen Kane

See *Heart of Darkness*.

Clean, Mr Clean

A teenage gunner (also known as **Bubba**) on the **PBR** played by **Larry** (now **Laurence) Fishburne**. **Willard** says: 'The crew were mostly just kids – rock 'n' rollers with one foot in their graves . . . Clean, Mr Clean, was from some South Bronx shit-hole and I think the light and space of **Vietnam** really put the zap on his head.' Willard (and **Michael Herr**) had come across so many of the typical enlisted American soldiers in Vietnam – young, badly out of place, getting stoned to cope.

The young Fishburne clearly brought an authentic inexperience and naivety to the role. He said on the set:

> The whole thing is really funny. I mean the war is funny. Shit, you can do anything you want to. That's why Vietnam must have been so much fun for the guys that were out there. I mean like I knows this one dude who came back, shit, and he's nothing but a dope-smoker and all he does is smoke dope and he said, 'Vietnam was the best thing they could have done to my ass.'

Fifteen years later, he had lost any sense of wide-eyed excitement:

I was just a kid. And that's what I think my role is about. It's about all the kids that were over there, you know, who didn't know anything about anything and they were just kinda snatched up and used as cannon fodder for this war.

As the boat progresses from **Do Long bridge** towards **Kurtz**'s compound, **Chef** reads a letter from his wife while Clean plays the tape that his mother has sent him. The voice on the tape is that of Fishburne's own mother, Hattie James. Moments later, Clean is killed in a fire-fight. Afterwards, as **Chief**, Willard and Chef tend to Clean's body, the tape is still running and we hear his mother's stilted voice saying how much she loves him, and telling him to 'stay out of the way of the bullets' and bring his 'hiney home all in one piece'. This is the film's one moment of tenderness and sentimentality (barring the relationship between **Lance** and the fateful **puppy**) and re-emphasises the sacrifice of youth in a conflict in which, famously, the average combatant was 19 years old.

The excision of the **French plantation** sequence robs the film of Clean's funeral.

His name may be an ironic reference to his **drug** consumption ('clean' meaning, among other things, free from drugs) or simply to his personal hygiene, as he is first seen brushing his teeth.

Clément, Aurore

French actress who made her acting début in Louis Malle's *Lacombe: Lucien*. She played the woman in the **French plantation** sequence who smokes opium with and beds **Willard**. This sequence was removed entirely from the release version. She is married to *Apocalypse Now*'s production designer, **Dean Tavoularis**.

Colby, Captain Richard

The man previously sent by the Corporation to kill **Kurtz**, played by

Scott Glenn. From his final communication from **Nha Trang**, before meeting Kurtz, **Willard** reads: 'Months ago a man was ordered on a mission which was identical to yours. We have reason to believe that he is now operating with Colonel Kurtz.' Colby was reported missing in action, but then a letter to his wife was intercepted:

> SELL The HOUSE
> SELL The CAR
> SELL The KIDS
> FIND SOMEONE ELSE
> I'M <u>NEVER</u> COMING ~~HOME~~ BACK
> FORGET IT!!!

When Willard confronts him as he enters the compound, the suspicions are confirmed. Like **Lance**, he is daubed with some idiosyncratic face **camouflage**, he has apparently been rendered mute (unlike **Dennis Hopper**'s **photo-journalist**, sadly) and he clasps his rifle in recently bloodied hands.

Colby seems to be inspired by the Dane Fresleven, **Marlow**'s forerunner in *Heart of Darkness*. As Marlow explains, 'I got my appointment – of course; and I got it very quick. It appears **the Company** had received news that one of their captains had been killed in a scuffle with the natives. This was my chance.' Colby is a final vivid warning, and yet after reading this letter and the death of **Clean** and **Chief**, Willard must meet Kurtz: 'I knew the risks or imagined I knew. But the thing I felt most, much stronger than fear, was the desire to confront him.'

In the mythical **five-hour version**, Colby's role is apparently increased to a twenty-minute cameo, concluding with him 'shot-gunning' the photo-journalist. As **Richard Marks** recalls, 'There was a whole sub-plot at the **temple** in which Willard tries to talk Colby into siding with him to get Kurtz. But it had to go because it wasn't wholly realised. It was never fully shot. It's sad what has to go.'

Colonel, the

The character jokingly named Colonel G. Lucas, played by **Harrison Ford**.

Se **Nha Trang**.

colonialism

Colonialism and its corruptive power provide the context for the journeys in *Apocalypse Now* and **Heart of Darkness**. **Conrad** was writing at the turn of the twentieth century when much of Africa, South America and Asia, having been divvied up, were still under the control of a handful of European countries. In his story it is specifically ivory that is the chief resource by which **Kurtz** is making money for **the Company**. Conrad has **Marlow** express his contempt for expansionism succinctly: 'The conquest of the earth . . . is not a pretty thing when you think about it too much.'

There is no such overt political comment (beyond **Willard**'s comment on the US generals' ineptitude) in the final version of *Apocalypse Now*, although there was a slightly didactic speech in the **French plantation** scene. What is implied is that Kurtz is an almost logical product of America's policy. The Americans initially expanded their sphere of influence into Indo-China for various reasons – all linked to its tactical geographical position. It was occupied by Japan from 1941, and then from 1949, after the Chinese Revolution, the Americans assisted the French in their struggle against the Vietminh. This assistance gradually increased, until by the mid-1950s the USA was the chief defender of the independence of the newly formed South **Vietnam**. Loosely speaking, one can see that colonialism, in the form of America's 'manifest destiny' – which cast it as an international protector against the spread of communism, specifically the feared domino effect in South-east Asia – led to the increase of American military influence in the area and ultimately to the **Vietnam War**.

Company, the

In *Heart of Darkness* **Joseph Conrad** was recreating a Congo journey that he himself had made as a young man. For the purposes of his novella, Conrad had to remove the real and specific names. The line between the physical and metaphorical journey becomes blurred partly because of the generic renaming of the employers and the stops on the unnamed river – Company Station, Central Station and Inner Station. **Marlow** seeks and gains employment from the Company, 'a big concern . . . [which] trade[s] on that river'.

In Conrad 'the Company' refers to the corporations privately owned by the Belgian King Leopold II which ran the Congo. Later, the Company was used as a euphemism for the CIA. The CIA and its predecessor the OSS were the pioneers of American involvement in **Vietnam** and had retained their influence, leading raids and reconnaissance missions into Cambodia, up to the time of the film's (presumed) setting, 1969. So it is an appropriate and neat device for **Willard** to be recruited to terminate **Kurtz**'s command by the similarly blankly named **COMSEC** and the Corporation, which seems to refer to the general American force, incorporating both the CIA and the military.

Coming Home

Film of 1979, directed by Hal Ashby, starring Jane Fonda, Jon Voight and Bruce Dern. Part of the wave of **Vietnam War films** to be produced by Hollywood studios in the late 1970s. It is the third of an informal trilogy with *Apocalypse Now* and *The Deer Hunter*. Were Oscars a true measure of cinematic quality, it would have to be judged a superior film to *Apocalypse Now*, as it won the awards for Best Actor, Best Actress and Best Original Screenplay.

Jane Fonda was a heroic/notorious, certainly vociferous opponent of America's continued military involvement in **Vietnam**. She travelled to Hanoi during the war, posing for a famous photograph on top of a North Vietnamese tank, and continually spoke out against American policy. This film started out when Fonda approached screenwriter Nancy Dowd with the idea of constructing a story that condemned America's role in Vietnam. It emerges as a simplistic, sentimental melodrama, with Jane Fonda playing a conventional army wife and nurse who, with the help of paraplegic 'Nam vet John Voight, discovers the orgasm, gets a frizzy hair-do and all in all (as she does in so many of her films) magically metamorphoses into Jane Fonda.

COMSEC I Corps

As **Willard** is being interviewed at headquarters in **Nha Trang** before receiving his mission, **the Colonel** runs through the dossier on his covert, unacknowledged activities: 'Your report specifies intelligence/counter-intelligence with COMSEC I Corps.'

COMSEC is short for Communications Security (there was also OPSEC – Operations Security). It was (still is) responsible for, among other things, the interception of enemy signals. I (or Eye) Corps refers to the northern part of South **Vietnam**. South Vietnam was divided into four corps areas from north to south, 1 to 4. 1 became I, and so Eye. Willard is engaged on the **Kurtz** mission by COMSEC 2 Corps.

Conrad, Joseph (1857–1924)

Jozef Teodor Konrad Korzeniowski was born into a prosperous family in Russian Poland. His politically active parents were both dead before Conrad entered his teens. At 17 he left Poland for Marseilles, from where he ran guns to Spain. This marked the beginning of twenty years of professional maritime adventures. He travelled over much of the world – the Mediterranean, the Far East, the West Indies and Africa – becoming a master mariner in the Polish Merchant Marines. He adopted British nationality in 1886, began his first novel, *Almayer's Folly*, in 1889 and finally retired from seafaring in 1894.

Although his talent was soon recognised, it was many years before he achieved any real financial success. But the few years leading up to his sudden death in 1924 saw him enjoy a measure of prosperity. Interestingly, much of this success came from film sales and options. His novels include *Youth*, *Lord Jim*, *Nostromo*, *The Secret Agent* and *Under Western Eyes*.

Much of his fiction was based on his experiences at sea. **Heart of Darkness** is certainly inspired by his journey up the Congo river in 1890, by which stage he had already embarked on his second career as a novelist in his third language, English (after Polish and French). He had been contracted to serve as an officer on river steamboats for the Société Anonyme pour le Commerce du Haut-Congo, owned by Leopold II, the exploitative Belgian king. Presumably this title led Conrad to give **Marlow**'s employers in *Heart of Darkness* the anonymous title **the Company**. He recorded the time he spent in the Congo in what came to be known as 'The Congo Diary', which constitutes the first known writing he undertook in English. This consisted of his brief reminiscences and his 'Up-river Book', in which he noted the physical appearance of the river, its changing depth and undulating course.

The writing is on the whole functional, presumably intended to serve later as a brief reminder of the time and the look of the country, but there are elements in these journals that prefigure incidents in *Heart of Darkness*. A possibly fanciful example is his description of a fight between a government employee and carriers in Nselemba. He says, 'Blows with sticks raining hard. Stopped it.' It is conceivable that on returning to these notes ten years later Conrad may have been struck by the image of 'sticks raining hard' and transposed it in its literal sense

into his narrative with the shower of **arrows** coming down upon the
steamer, a sequence which survives virtually intact in *Apocalypse Now*.
Perhaps not.

What is certain is that several key moments in Conrad's life – his
journey up the Congo and subsequent illness, disillusionment and
depression – informed the novel. Marlow's boyhood desires to travel
and specifically to explore Central Africa in the footsteps of Stanley
are precisely Conrad's own. On the journey itself, Conrad was not
the captain but merely an observer. At Stanley Falls, the Inner Station
of the novel, they had to collect the French agent, Georges Antoine
Klein, who was very sick with dysentery. He died on the return
journey to Kinshasa (the Central Station) and was buried at Bolobo.
This provided the structure of the story rather than the character of
Kurtz (and the character was initially named Klein), who seems to
have been loosely based on another Company agent called Hodister,
an enlightened explorer whose death in 1892 was reported in English
newspapers.

Writing from Stanley Falls in September 1890, Conrad expressed
his deep disappointment at arriving at this place that had possessed
near-mythical importance and attraction in his childhood: 'A great
melancholy descended upon me. Yes this was the very spot.' But what
he found was the

'distasteful knowledge of the vilest scramble for loot that ever
disfigured the history of human conscience and geographical
exploration. What an end to the idealised realities of a boy's
daydreams! . . . Still, the fact remains that I have smoked a pipe
of peace at midnight in the very heart of the African continent,
and felt very lonely there.'

Conrad returned to Belgium from the Congo suffering from the
effects of dysentery and feeling generally demoralised. This mood, the
atmosphere, these real events and characters fed the nascent writer's

imagination, and emerged altered but recognisable in *Heart of Darkness* and subsequently in *Apocalypse Now*.

Coppola, Carmine (1910–91)

Composer/musician, father of **Francis (Ford) Coppola**, born in New York to Italian immigrant parents. Won a flute scholarship to the Juilliard School in New York. There is a character in *The Godfather Part II*, based on him as a young boy, who plays the flute for a gunsmith (the character is actually called Carmine Coppola). He played with the Detroit Symphony Orchestra, then as first flute in the NBC Symphony Orchestra under Arturo Toscanini. After a variety of musical jobs, his first collaboration with his son (apart from the music he wrote for Coppola's debut nudie picture *Tonight For Sure*) came when Francis invited him to help with the orchestration for *Finian's Rainbow*. He went on to write additional music for *The Godfather*, and conducted Nino Rota's score for *The Godfather Part II*, before co-composing with Francis the haunting electronic soundtrack music for *Apocalypse Now*.

In 1980 Francis Coppola bought the distribution rights to Abel Gance's silent classic *Napoleon*, which Kevin Brownlow had restored to its original triptych form. In certain venues Coppola controversially rejected the score that Carl Davis had written using scraps of material from the original accompaniment, and replaced it with a live soundtrack composed and conducted by Carmine. He also wrote the music for *The Outsiders*, *Gardens of Stone*, *Life Without Zoe* from *New York Stories* and *The Godfather Part III*. Francis Coppola has often been criticised for his nepotism. He has employed in various capacities his wife, father, brother, sister, son, daughter and nephew. Usually his decisions have paid off, and the use of his father as composer has been well justified, particularly in his memorable contributions to *The Godfather* and *Apocalypse Now*.

See **soundtrack**.

Coppola, Eleanor

Née Neil. Artist, writer and film-maker born in Los Angeles, California. She graduated from the Art Department of UCLA (the University of California at Los Angeles) and met Coppola while working as assistant to the art director on *Dementia 13*, which Coppola directed for Roger Corman. They both worked on another Corman film, *The Terror*, before they were married, on 2 February 1963 in Las Vegas, and she moved into semi-retired domesticity. They have had three children, Gian-Carlo (who died in an accident in 1986), Roman and Sofia. Between 1976 and 1979 she kept a diary, which was published in 1979 as *Notes*: *On the Making of Apocalypse Now*. This provides many fascinating insights into the conditions on the set, as well as being an account of the near break-up of her marriage, which was threatened by the stress of the shoot and her husband's affair. She was also engaged to shoot film for a 'making-of' documentary. The footage she shot formed the basis of **Hearts of Darkness: A Filmmaker's Apocalypse**, which also featured interview material with her and her reading from *Notes*.

Coppola, Francis (Ford) (b. 1939)

Director, producer, writer and composer born in Detroit, Michigan. He suffered from polio as a child. He studied drama at Hofstra University before entering films (like so many others – Jonathan Demme, **Jack Nicholson**, Martin Scorsese, Peter Bogdanovich, *et al.*) working for the genius of exploitation, Roger Corman, who is jokily and subliminally referred to in the film in the character of **General Corman**. Coppola's debut was the nudie film *Tonight For Sure*, which he followed up with a cheapo horror film, the meaninglessly titled *Dementia 13*. He plodded through a series of unremarkable films as director – *You're A Big Boy Now*, *Finian's Rainbow* and *The Rain People* – while doing more interesting and distinguished work on scripts for other film-makers – *Is Paris Burning?*, *This Property is Condemned* and *Patton*, for which he shared the Oscar for best adapted screenplay with Edmund H. North.

As a man of many interests and with a passion for control, for overseeing other people's projects, and most especially wanting to establish and be a part of a creative group of diverse artists and film-makers, Coppola formed American **Zoetrope** in 1969. This idealistic company was launched with seed money provided by Warner-Seven Arts and, in a different guise, survives to the present. Among its early projects were **George Lucas**'s dystopian sci-fi vision *THX 1138*, his splendid, highly successful and influential teen-film *American Graffiti* and **John Milius**'s original screenplay for *Apocalypse Now*.

For a variety of reasons – talent, rich creative collaborations encompassing writing, design, **lighting**, camera work, costume, **sound, music, editing,** consistently impeccable casting and acting, choice of subject matter, enthusiasm, ambition, passion and luck – the 1960s marked a period of quite remarkable artistic and commercial achievement for Coppola. *The Godfather* is a near-flawless film. It has since been claimed that the film was chaotic in preparation and was largely shaped in post-production. Nevertheless, what emerged is one of the most brilliantly realised films ever made. It shows the idealised gangster family, the Corleones (famously never referred to as 'mafia' or '*cosa nostra*'), as representations of the American dream and simultaneously as figures from a modern Greek tragedy unable to escape from their determined roles.

The Godfather Part II is the antithesis of the modern sequel, as it comments on and implicitly criticises rather than reiterates the original. Where *The Godfather* was smooth and exhilarating, its sequel is confused, complex and depressing. It traces the origins of the Corleone crime dynasty to the petty, violent feuds of Sicily and the small steps, leading inevitably to a life of crime, taken by the young immigrant Vito in New York's Little Italy. These scenes are juxtaposed with the continuing descent of his son Michael, who faces the consequences of his and his father's profession. While the family business continues to prosper, he destroys – he has already destroyed – everything, his wife, his family, himself.

These two films both won the Academy Award for the best film of their respective years. In the nominations for Best Director in the 1974 awards, Coppola achieved the still unmatched feat of being nominated twice – for *The Godfather Part II* and his previous film *The Conversation*. Though the latter was much smaller in scale, and a commercial failure, it is another great film, a brilliant, disorienting exploration of isolation, misinterpretation and paranoia. Perhaps most importantly, it is a film about sound, and the sound editor on this film was **Walter Murch**, an under-acknowledged creative force behind Coppola's rich vein of success in his golden era.

John Milius wrote the original screenplay for *Apocalypse Now* in 1969. Several times it came close to being made with George Lucas as director. After these various false starts, Coppola took over the project as director. He immediately adopted the plan that Lucas had developed, to shoot the film in **the Philippines**. Coppola's intention from the beginning was 'to take the audience through an unprecedented experience of war and have them react as much as those who had gone through the war'. This declaration is characteristic of his role as entrepreneur and showman hyping his own product, but it also reveals the impossible ambition which would drive him over the next three years to endanger other people's lives, his own recently amassed fortune, his marriage and his sanity.

He echoed and expanded upon these ambitions when he presented the film in 1979:

> The most important thing I wanted to do in the making of *Apocalypse Now* was to create a film experience that would give its audience a sense of the **horror**, the madness, the sensuousness, and the moral dilemma of the **Vietnam War**.

When I began work on the film, over four years ago, I thought it was going to be the only American feature film made dealing with the war, and so I worked with that in mind. I tried to illustrate as many of its different facets as possible. And yet I wanted it to go further, to the moral issues that are behind all wars.

Over the period of shooting, this film gradually made itself; and curiously, the process of making the film became very much like the story of the film.

I found that many of the ideas and images with which I was working as a film director began to coincide with the realities of my own life, and that I, like **Captain Willard**, was moving up a river in a faraway **jungle**, looking for answers and hoping for some kind of catharsis.

It was my thought that if the American audience could look at the heart of what **Vietnam** was really like – what it looked like and felt like – then they would be only one small step away from putting it behind them.

It is statements like these, complementing his films, that make Coppola so fascinating a character. This is in the same spirit as John Milius's original and insane plan to shoot the film in Vietnam in the midst of the war (in 1969) – or rather, as George Lucas pointed out, to have George Lucas and the crew shoot the film in Vietnam. However, this itself emerges as part of the background myth to the film, according to Walter Murch, with the plan being to travel no further than the Sacramento Delta to make the film.

Still, this betrays a certain degree of ego and bravado – the hype of the Barnum that Coppola partly was. But, as when dealing with his speech after the first screening in **Cannes**, we must give him some credit for sincerity. He is sincerely mad. Taking him at face value when he says that this isn't a movie, this is war, this is Vietnam, that, as he himself confessed and **Eleanor Coppola** noted during the shooting, he identified with both Willard (probably insane) and **Kurtz** (definitively and 'obviously insane'), leads to this odd conclusion. As David Cronenberg has had to point out on many occasions in his defence against accusations about the danger of the violent images and ideas in his films, particularly *Crash*, 'to confuse reality and art is the definition of psychosis'. This is a confusion that Coppola seems to have wilfully courted. As a Hitchcockian cameo appearance, and at the same time playing on his role as impresario and emphasising the blurred distinction between fiction and reality, Coppola is seen on the beach when Willard and the **PBR** crew first encounter **Kilgore** and his **Air Cavalry**, playing a newsreel director, with **Vittorio Storaro** as his cameraman. He shouts at Willard: 'Don't look at the camera. Just go by like you're fighting, like you're fighting. It's for television.'

He emerged from this experience apparently unchastened. **Martin Sheen** survived, the Coppolas' marriage survived, Francis Coppola's reputation and wealth were, against all the odds and all predictions, even enhanced. So he chose to make a romantic musical, with non-bankable leads, recreating large areas of Las Vegas on two-thirds scale in a studio, and, as with *Apocalypse Now*, most of the money he staked on this extremely risky venture was his own. As Stephen Bach – the Head of Production at **United Artists** at the time of *Apocalypse Now*'s completion, author of the excellent *Final Cut* and avowed admirer of Coppola – has pointed out, Coppola 'has gone to the edge of the cliff several times, jumped and landed safely for whatever reasons, partly luck'. He didn't land safely with *One From the Heart*, and this had little to do with luck but more with that feature of *The Godfather* films, hubris.

After the trials of *Apocalypse*, there seem retrospectively to be two deep forces at work in Coppola's career – a feeling of his own infallibility combined with other people's suspicion that he was a spent force. Having been to the heart of darkness, where could he go now? It is quite possible to make an aesthetic defence of *One From the Heart*. It is a dazzling film, enhanced if not rendered worthwhile by the extraordinary design and camera work supplied by **Dean Tavoularis** and Vittorio Storaro, who had provided the stunning visuals for *Apocalypse Now*. It isn't quite empty and worthless, but it is essentially light. It is in the same bracket as two other notoriously profligate films of the budget-reviewing age, *Ishtar* and *Waterworld*. They are all small, even B-films that have been allotted inappropriate, disproportionate budgets.

Many of the films Coppola has directed in his post-*Apocalypse* period have apparently been undertaken out of commercial necessity. This explains but doesn't excuse his decision to make *The Godfather Part III*. It is unfair to claim that Coppola's talent has been wholly wasted since *Apocalypse Now*. He has produced some worthwhile films, including *The Black Stallion*, directed by Carroll Ballard, who nearly brought **Heart of Darkness** to the screen in 1967; *Hammett* and *Mishima*. Also his own films have not been totally without interest, most notably *Rumblefish*, which is *nearly* great. He has fostered some valuable collaborations – with the already mentioned Dean Tavoularis, Vittorio Storaro and Walter Murch, but also with actors such as **Robert Duvall**, **Al Pacino**, **Frederic Forrest** and **Dennis Hopper** (at times when few directors would work with him). He has a remarkable record for spotting young acting talent, giving early breaks to, among others, Diane Keaton, **Laurence Fishburne**, Nicolas Cage and, in *The Outsiders* alone, Matt Dillon, Rob Lowe, Tom Cruise, Patrick Swayze, Ralph Macchio, Diane Lane, C. Thomas Howell and Emilio Estevez, Martin Sheen's son. He is also a serious wine-maker.

As is shown most vividly by the example of *Apocalypse Now*, Coppola emerges as a unique kind of mad method director. He was not reluctant to show himself as having lived the film, lived and recreated the war, confronted the darkness, the madness, the evil. He revealed and revelled in his own ego and megalomania. He is simultaneously the embodiment and contradiction of the *auteur* theory – the film is ultimately his own vision and yet clearly the product of so many diverse contributions. You get the strong impression that after this extraordinary run of gambles from *The Godfather* to *One From the Heart*, which mainly paid off artistically and commercially, he no longer would or could stake so much of himself on any project. But *Apocalypse Now* stands as a fitting climax to a decade of remarkable creativity.

Corman, General

In the scene in which the unnamed **Colonel** is in fact called Colonel G. Lucas, the unnamed **General** is called Corman, after **Coppola**'s early employer Roger Corman, the king of the exploitation film. Corman himself makes a walk-on appearance in *The Godfather Part II*, and has played similar cameos in the films of some of his other protégés, including Jonathan Demme's *The Silence of the Lambs* and Ron Howard's *Apollo 13*.

cost

The film was budgeted at $12 million. It is difficult to ascertain a precise figure for how much the production cost, as it is variously reported to have been $30 million, $30.5 million, $31 million and $31.5 million. A reasonable consensus suggests that the film was completed for approximately $30.5 million. It is difficult to find precise box-office figures for the film, but it is stated in **Hearts of Darkness: A Filmmaker's Apocalypse** that the film grossed more than $100 million world-wide.

'Crock O' BLIP! Now, A'

Spoof of *Apocalypse Now* in July 1980 issue of *MAD* Magazine.

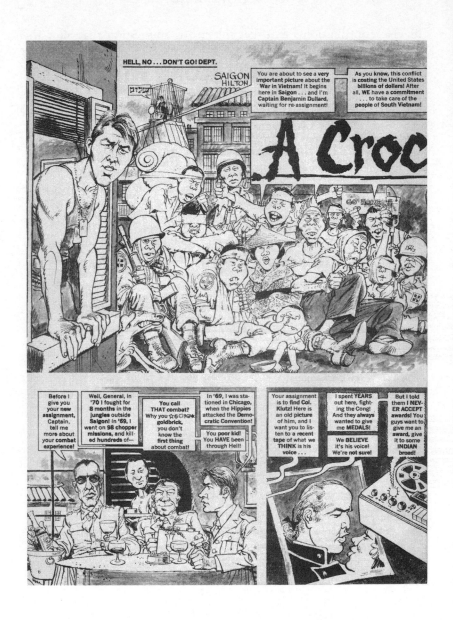

WRITER: LARRY SIEGEL

D

date

See **Manson, Charles Milles**.

death cards

In the aftermath of the **Air Cavalry**'s first rogue raid **Colonel Kilgore** walks from corpse to corpse dealing each one a playing card:

KILGORE: Let's see what we have. Two of spades, three of spades, four of diamonds, six of clubs, eight of spades. There isn't one with a jack in the whole bunch.
LANCE: Hey, Captain, what's that?
WILLARD: Death Cards.
LANCE: What?
WILLARD: Death Cards. Lets **Charlie** know who did this.

This, like all the other unlikely, fantastic military activity, is based in fact. In Peter Cowie's **Coppola**, **Michael Herr**

> recalls that, after an ambush that had killed several Americans, the **Viet Cong** 'covered the field with copies of a photograph that showed one more young, dead American, with the punch line mimeographed on the back, "Your X-rays have just come back from the lab and we think we know what your problem is."'

In *Vietnam Inc.* Philip Jones Griffiths also has captions to some grisly photographs of dead Viet Cong soldiers which read:

> Men of the 'Tropic Lightning', the 25th Infantry Division, leave their 'Visiting cards' – torn-off shoulder patches depicting the division's emblem, a bolt of lightning – stuffed in the mouths of people they kill.

decapitation

Chef is the final victim of **Kurtz**'s penchant for beheading. After their first foray into the compound, Chef says to **Willard**, 'I used to think that if I died in an evil place, then my soul wouldn't be able to make it to heaven', so he would be upset to learn that his **head**'s final resting place was Willard's lap. Elaine Zablotny argues that this scene is one of the subliminal castration images that pepper the film.

See **balls**.

Deer Hunter, The

Film directed by Michael Cimino in 1978 starring Robert De Niro, Christopher Walken, John Cazale, John Savage and Meryl Streep, another of the early wave of high-profile Hollywood **Vietnam War films**. Like *Coming Home*, it highlights the epic struggle to bring *Apocalypse Now* to the screen; it was conceived after *Apocalypse* began shooting but released a year before it. The story is divided into three parts. In the long prologue the characters of the working-class Russian-Americans are established as they attend a wedding, drink and go hunting before three of them go off to **Vietnam**. The middle section sees them at war, captured and, in the film's central and most famous sequence, forced to play Russian roulette. Walken can't leave **Saigon**, Savage returns home a cripple and De Niro is deeply disturbed.

Where *Coming Home* is bad melodrama, *The Deer Hunter* is a good, possibly even great, melodrama. There is a certain over-blown quality to the film; it is somewhat crude but undeniably powerful, and is beautifully acted. Whether or not it is possible to counter the accusations of **racism**, it is certainly controversial in its handling of history. This questioning of the historical basis of a central aspect of the story is something that *The Deer Hunter* shares with *Apocalypse Now*. In the latter film, the event that is shown to have been a, if not the main, revelation of the horror of war for **Kurtz** and a catalyst in his descent into madness is the story of the dismemberment of **polio**-vaccinated Vietnamese children. Many have claimed that this is pure fiction, although **John Milius** asserts that this was witnessed by his friend **Fred Rexer**. Likewise, many people have criticised Michael Cimino for the harrowing Russian roulette scenes, saying that they are not based on historical events. Cimino, whose ego is no less rampant than **Coppola**'s, seemed deliberately to confuse the argument and controversy by insisting sometimes that there were known cases of the **Viet Cong** organising these games, at other times that they were neither based on fact nor served a metaphorical purpose, they were merely there.

From Coppola's point of view, the real effect of *The Deer Hunter* and *Coming Home* was that they changed the atmosphere into which his film would be released. He felt at the start of the project that he might be making the only American film about the **Vietnam War**. While the two predecessors proved that films dealing directly with the war could be not only controversial but commercially and critically successful, they and the many films that followed set up an informal competition for which was the best, most authentic evocation of the Vietnam experience.

With splendid irony, Coppola found himself at the 1979 **Academy**

Award ceremony handing the Oscar for Best Film to Michael Cimino
for *The Deer Hunter.*

dialectics

In the **temple**, while **Kurtz** reads aloud from **T. S. Eliot**'s *The
Hollow Men*, the **photo-journalist** confides in **Willard**:

> 'Oh, he's out there. He's really out there. Do you hear what
> the man's saying? Do you? This is dialectics. It's very simple
> dialectics. One through nine. No maybes, no supposes, no
> fractions. You can't travel in space, you can't go into space,
> you know, without, er, you know, with fractions. What are
> you going to land on? One quarter? Three eighths? What are
> you going to do when you go from here to Venus or something?
> That's dialectic physics. Dialectic logic is there's only love and
> hate. You either love someone or you hate 'em.'

Kurtz suddenly throws a book at him, presumably not entirely
satisfied with his definition of complex philosophical notions. The
photographer bows out of the scene and the film saying, 'This is the
way the fucking world ends. Look at this fucking shit we're in, man.
Not with a bang, but with a whimper. And with a whimper I'm
fucking splitting, jack.' So, with a near quotation of the last line of
The Hollow Men ('Not with a bang but a whimper'), ends the oddity
that is **Dennis Hopper**'s performance.

dink

In **Kilgore**'s **napalm** speech he talks of the aftermath of the hail-
bomb, when he couldn't find 'one stinking dink body' on the whole
hill. Dink was a common nickname for the **Viet Cong**. As **Michael
Herr** recalls in *Dispatches*:

> A bird colonel, commanding a brigade of the 4th Infantry

Division: 'I'll bet you always wondered why we call 'em Dinks up in this part of the country. I thought of it myself. I'll tell you, I never *did* like hearing them called **Charlie**. See, I had an uncle named Charlie, and I liked him too. No, Charlie was just too damn good for the little bastards. So I just thought, What are they *really* like? And I came up with rinky-dink. Suits 'em just perfect, Rinky-Dink. 'Cept that was too long, so we cut it down some. And that's why we call 'em Dinks.'

In fact, the use of the term, from the rhyming mentioned here, for East and South-east Asians was recorded as early as 1938.

director's cut

This is an elusive, mythical version of the film that, according to *Film Threat* magazine, does exist in some form. It isn't actually the director's cut, as that is the film that is generally seen and known. It is instead a version of the film approximating that shown to various groups of friends, colleagues, **United Artists** and Paramount representatives, members of the press and the public in several screenings from April 1978 to the near-final version shown at the **Cannes Film Festival** in 1979. During this period the film was whittled down from a seven-and-a-half-hour version (actually three and a half hours of material up to **Kurtz**'s compound and four hours at the compound) to the final length of around two and a half hours.

There is something enormously appealing about the idea of the director's cut of one's favourite films, and they have become a minor trend of the last twenty years. There have been reissues supervised by the director of, among others, *Close Encounters of the Third Kind*, *Heaven's Gate*, *Blade Runner*, *Betty Blue* and *The Big Blue*. While sometimes they include odd restored scenes, lengthy passages, even occasional deletions, they are by no means universally improvements Of the films mentioned above, *Close Encounters* is marginally enhanced by the trimming of longueurs and the restoration of a couple of scenes, *Betty Blue* makes a little more sense in this version, but *Blade Runner* is harmed by the removal of the voice-over and god knows why anyone would want more of *The Big Blue*.

There is that simple desire for more of a good thing, but in the case of *Apocalypse Now* what seems chaotic and confused on first viewing is of course carefully honed and pared down. In theory, with the hours of improvised material with the crew of the **PBR**, **Marlon Brando**, **Dennis Hopper** and others, and **the French plantation** sequence, the film could have been three times as long, but it would have been less good.

See **five-hour version**.

Disneyland

The morning after the boat leaves **Do Long bridge**, **Lance** reads a letter from a friend who says, 'There could never be a place like Disneyland or could there? Let me know.' Lance says, 'Jim, it's here. It really is here.' He concludes that **Vietnam** is even 'better than Disneyland'.

This isn't just a manifestation of Lance's madness. The scene is juxtaposed with **Chef** reading about **Charles Manson**, and these are clearly the extremes of American culture as reflected in Vietnam. There is the weird contrast throughout the film of icons of American culture (**Playboy Bunnies**, beach parties, **Beverly Hills**, Disneyland, mass murderers) exported to Vietnam. In *Heart of Darkness* **Kurtz** goes mad in a desolate place because of the barbarity of civilisation. In *Apocalypse Now* he goes mad 'in that old crazy Asian war' because he is fulfilling his duty.

The idea behind this scene is presumably to present the **Vietnam War** as a theme park designed by a murderous psychopath, in the context of a film centring around the quest for a man called Walt.

Dispatches

A book that took **Michael Herr** seven years to distil from the various pieces that he had written for *Esquire*, *Rolling Stone* and *New American Review*. It is a brilliant, vivid evocation of the experience of the **Vietnam War** and was one of the chief influences on *Apocalypse Now*. **John Milius** has said that when he originally wrote the script one of his main sources was *'The Battle for Khe Sanh'*, an article which forms the central section of *Dispatches*. Michael Herr's style comes through strongly in the **voice-over** which he wrote, but the book as a whole clearly shaped the attitude of the film. This is partly down to the fact that both seem to capture some authentic essence of the war. But Michael Herr was really there, got continually really scared and really stoned. He was among the first to capture **Vietnam** as a **rock 'n' roll war**, where young soldiers listened with reverence to **Hendrix**, took **drugs**, fought, went insane and died. Some details and some larger events have been transferred almost directly from book to film. They share the same slang, the same attitude and the general feeling of the disillusionment of the ordinary soldier trapped in a distant war being waged with no coherent, workable strategy. It is a great book openly declaring its moral ambiguity and its author's ambivalent feelings about the war, as essential to *Apocalypse Now* as **Heart of Darkness**.

Do Long bridge

Referred to by the crew as the 'Gates of Hell' sequence – one of the most surreal episodes of the film, though in fact quite closely based on real events. The bridge itself is the outpost of official American involvement, presumably close to but not on the Cambodian border. It is described as being rebuilt every day only to be blown up again every night. This Sisyphean task symbolises the pointlessness of many of the engagements of the real war, with time, effort and lives expended in the desperate attempt to gain, regain or retain territory from an enemy whose criteria for success and victory were so different from their own. The bridge used was, as **Coppola** says, 'erected by the crew on pilings of an old span that had been demolished in World War II, washed away in the typhoon and was reconstructed in order to be destroyed for the film'.

This sequence is the one that bears closest resemblance to **'The Battle for Khe Sanh'** from **Michael Herr**'s *Dispatches*. The chaos of the besieged, leaderless Americans huddled terrified in the trenches as the action is lit stroboscopically by dropping flares echoes Herr's descriptions:

> the sky beyond the western perimeter is burning with slowly dropping magnesium flares . . . It is a small trench, and a lot of us have gotten into it in a hurry. At the end farthest from me there is a young guy who has been hit in the throat, and he is making the sounds a baby will make when he is trying to make up the breath for a good scream.

As **Willard** and **Lance** progress through the trenches they come across a couple of soldiers firing a fixed machine-gun at the one remaining **Viet Cong** soldier at the wire, who is screaming almost non-stop. A third soldier approaches, whose bearing is psychotically calm. The machine-gunner turns to him and asks:

> 'You hear him out there by the wire, man?'
> 'Yeah.'
> 'You need a flare?'
> 'No. He's close man, real close.'

He aims and adjusts his hand-held M-16 grenade launcher and fires. With the explosion, the screaming stops dead. He says, 'Fucker.' Willard asks him if he knows who is in charge, and he replies 'Yeah', before slipping back into darkness.

This is clearly a re-enactment of the scene that Herr relates from his time at Khe Sanh:

We heard then what sounded at first like a little girl crying, a
subdued, delicate wailing, and as we listened it became louder
and more intense, taking on pain as it grew until it was a full
piercing shriek. . . . '**Slope**,' Mayhew said. 'See him there, see
there, on the wire there?' I couldn't see anything out there,
there was no movement, and the screaming had stopped. As the
flare dimmed, the sobbing started up and built quickly until it
was a scream again.

A Marine brushed past us. He had a moustache and a piece
of camouflaged parachute silk fastened bandanna-style around
his throat, and on his hip he wore a holster which held an M-79
grenade launcher. For a second I thought I'd hallucinated him.
I hadn't heard him approaching, and I tried now to see where
he might have come from, but I couldn't. The M-79 had been
cut down and fitted with a special stock. It was obviously a
well-loved object; you could see the kind of work that had
gone into it by the amount of light that caught from the
flares that glistened on the stock. The Marine looked serious,
dead-eyed serious, and his right hand hung above the holster,
waiting. The screaming had stopped again.

'Wait,' he said. 'I'll fix that fucker.'

His hand was resting now on the handle of the weapon. The
sobbing began again, and the screaming; we had the pattern now,
the North Vietnamese was screaming the same thing over and
over, and we didn't need a translator to tell us what it was.

'Put that fucker away,' the Marine said, as though to himself.
He drew the weapon, opened the breach and dropped a round
that looked like a great swollen bullet, listening very carefully
all the while to the shrieking. He placed the M-79 over his left
forearm and aimed for a second before firing. There was an
enormous flash on the wire 200 metres away, a spray of orange
sparks, and then everything was still except for the roll of some
bombs exploding kilometres away and the sound of the M-79

being opened, closed again and returned to the holster. Nothing changed on the Marine's face, nothing, and he moved back into the darkness.

The shooting of the Do Long bridge scenes was as intense and dreamlike as the action itself. As **Sam Bottoms** has confessed, he took a small cocktail of **dope**, speed and alcohol to enhance his performance – Lance has taken **acid**. In *Notes* **Eleanor Coppola** describes the magical atmosphere on the set:

> Maybe it was the fires that special effects started, and the arc lights illuminating the hundreds of extras in costume in the trenches. Maybe it was knowing that after all the rehearsing and preparing, this was it. There was a kind of electricity in the air. Parts seemed like a circus.

By the sixth day 'The circus mood was gone'. They struggled with the expensive special effects and heavy rain, and the crew's perfectionism meant further delays. On the eleventh night the camera was being set. The shot was a close-up on **Albert Hall**:

> There was a long discussion about whether Albert's look was supposed to be to camera right or camera left. The script supervisor was sure it was camera right, but **Vittorio** [**Storaro**, director of photography] thought it was camera left and wanted to shoot it both ways to be sure. **Jerry** [**Ziesmer**, assistant director and speaker of the immortal – and his only – line **'Terminate with extreme prejudice'**] said there wasn't time to do both. The exhaust smoke from the diesel engines was blowing on us. The evening began to look like just hard work.

Two days later, on 20 August 1976:

> It was supposed to be the last night of shooting at Do Long

Bridge. But it went very slowly. A day of delay means $30,000 to $50,000. This set has fallen behind two days. There are many grumbles about why. There are a lot of reasons. Sometimes the camera set-up seems slow, sometimes the special effects seem to take a long time to reload. Sometimes an actor needs more rehearsal. Sometimes **Francis [Coppola]** adds some new dialogue. Tonight Francis laid out a shot early in the evening and came home for about forty minutes to have a cup of soup while the **lighting** and dolly track were being set. It rained all the time he was home. When he got back to location, the river had risen nearly six feet. The scene was to be played with the actor walking along the bank through the mud to the boat. Now there was no bank, the scene had to be played with the guy wading waist deep in the water. Everything was slowed down; by midnight spirits were sagging as it became apparent that the evening's work was going to take another night.

Doors, the

Rock 'n' roll band of the late 1960s/early 1970s, led by charismatic, portly, self-indulgent boulevardier, ex-film student and bad poet Jim Morrison. Like **Coppola**, Morrison attended UCLA Film School. The Doors were clearly one of the bands popular among the grunts, as shown by Oliver Stone's example. Stone followed up *Platoon*, his semi-autobiographical-semi-remake of *Apocalypse Now*, with *The Doors*, in which he unwisely took at face value the self-mythologising of Jim Morrison and the Jim Morrison-mythologising of Danny Zuckerman. Still, the Doors were intermittently marvellous, they somehow capture their time, and with their strange Oedipal-fest **'The End'** they provide the perfect **soundtrack** brackets for the action.

They are cited as an important band in the soundtrack of **Vietnam** by **Michael Herr** in *Dispatches*. He talks of their 'distant, icy sound.

It seemed like such wintry music; you could rest your forehead against the window where the air conditioner had cooled the glass, close your eyes and feel the heat pressing against you from outside.' Herr also talks of how his Vietnam buddy Tim Page, one of the inspirations for **Hopper**'s **photo-journalist** character, got busted with the Doors in New Haven.

See **beginning, the**; **end, the**.

dope

See **marijuana**.

'Drop the bomb, exterminate them all'

Having killed **Kurtz** and assumed Kurtz's identity in **camouflage**, **Willard** has to decide what to do, and during shooting **Coppola** had to decide how to **end** the film, having early on in the project rejected **Milius**'s original idea of having Willard join the renegade **Green Berets** in a climactic battle with a **Viet Cong** battalion. Willard finds next to the typewriter Kurtz's memoirs (of which he literally becomes **caretaker**), and as he riffles the pages he finds that on one page Kurtz has scrawled over the text:

DROP

THE

BOMB

EXTERMINATE

THEM ALL!

With the ending as ambiguous (more than ambiguous in fact) as it is, it remains unclear whether Willard will obey this instruction. Coppola was presumably inspired by the conclusion of **Conrad**'s Kurtz's report for the International Society for the Suppression of Savage Customs, which **Marlow** reads while heading up river:

> 'It was very simple, and at the end of that moving appeal to every altruistic sentiment it blazed at you, luminous and terrifying, like a flash of lightning in a serene sky: "Exterminate all the brutes!"'

drugs

Drugs permeate the film. The crew of the **PBR** is constantly getting stoned and this mood seems to have been carried over into the shooting. **Sam Bottoms** has talked about how the crew was invited to the actors' party moving down the river. He has admitted that during the shoot he took speed, got stoned and dropped **acid**. There is a mood of hazy drugginess throughout the film, from the actors through the characters and often to the audience. I know of one person who, while taking an isolation cure from heroin addiction, had a checklist of essentials, like Renton in *Trainspotting*. The one luxury he allowed himself was a video of *Apocalypse Now*, which he watched repeatedly while going cold turkey.

George Lucas claimed that 'at the point when we were developing this, nobody knew that there were drugs over there'. But that can't be true. **Michael Herr**'s reports from the war, collated and modified in *Dispatches*, are filled with accounts of him and the soldiers around him getting stoned, and contains references to opium. Also there is documentation of the widespread use of drugs – chiefly **dope** and heroin – in several of the newsreel reports from the war. Reports at the time estimated that over half of the troops in **Vietnam** used **marijuana** and almost a third had experimented with opium and heroin.

The film's one scene of opium use was sadly lost as part of the **French plantation** sequence.

Duvall, Robert (b. 1931)

Actor, born in San Diego, California. His father was a rear-admiral, his mother an amateur actress. He studied drama at Principia College, Illinois. After two years in the army he moved to New York, where he studied acting and soon made an impact in off-Broadway productions. He developed into one of America's great character actors, and almost wilfully avoided stardom. In *Adventures in the Screen Trade* William Goldman praised his painfully honest performance in *The Great Santini*, to illustrate the difference between a film star and a character actor. No true star would allow himself to appear so unsympathetic on screen.

Although his choice of projects hasn't been impeccable, his acting has been, and his perfectly judged performances have added depth to bad and great films alike. From his film debut as Boo Radley in *To Kill a Mockingbird*, through *The Chase, Bullitt, True Grit, M*A*S*H*, to *The Great Northfield Minnesota Raid*, he made memorable, measured supporting contributions. In the 1980s and beyond he has continued to give notable performances, often in more substantial roles, particularly *Tender Mercies*, for which he won the Best Actor Oscar, *Colors, Falling Down, The Paper* and *The Apostle*, which brought him another Oscar nomination.

But it is the 1970s and particularly his collaborations with **Coppola** that define him and mark the highpoints (so far) of his career. He was good in *Rain People*, but quite remarkable in *The Godfather* and *The Godfather Part II*. He is brilliantly restrained as Tom Hagen, Vito Corleone's informally adopted son and *consigliere*. He made a highly effective, short, shocking, uncredited appearance in *The Conversation*, and followed these performances memorably as **Colonel Bill Kilgore** in *Apocalypse Now*. Gene Hackman was Coppola's first choice, and the fact that you can imagine him being very good in the role clearly takes nothing away from Duvall's achievement in the part. It is a great tribute to the writing as well as Duvall's acting that this mad, war-loving, xenophobic monster emerges as a rounded character — funny and pathetic as well as scary. The Kilgore sequence has been criticised for being almost too good, the character too charismatic, so as to unbalance the film. This is, I think, unfair and wrong, as Coppola still has up his sleeve the **tiger**, the **Playboy Bunnies**, the **sampan** and **Do Long bridge**, as well as **Dennis Hopper** and **Marlon Brando**. It is inevitable that the film has an air of loss, with the departure of such a huge character at the centre of beautifully orchestrated chaos, who signs off with one of the great speeches in film history. In fact Duvall's is among the greatest cameo performances in cinema.

E

E

Colonel Walter **Kurtz**'s middle initial, standing for nothing.

editing

See **Murch, Walter**; **Marks, Richard**.

Eliot, T. S. (1888–1965)

American-born English poet, playwright and critic. He is the central figure in the literary creation of the cinematic **Kurtz**, as shown through his library. It is his *The Hollow Men*, with its epigraph 'Mistah Kurtz – he dead', taken from **Conrad**'s *Heart of Darkness*, which Kurtz and the **photo-journalist** recite in the film. Equally important is the unspoken influence of Eliot's earlier work *The Waste Land*, to which Eliot initially planned to affix the epigraph **'The horror, the horror'**. This has a two-fold effect on the film. Its suggested presence (in Eliot's *Selected Poems*) in **Kurtz's library** implies that Kurtz has read it and empathises with its post-Great War mood of moral and spiritual desolation in the Western world and the spiritual continuum that links modern myths to those of Christianity, Hinduism, Buddhism and pagan rituals. This importance is emphasised by the presence on the shelf of **Jessie L. Weston**'s *From Ritual to Romance* and **J. G. Frazer**'s *The Golden Bough*, both of which Eliot cites as crucial influences in his own notes to *The Waste Land*. The central thread that links *From Ritual to Romance*, *The Waste Land* and *Apocalypse Now* is the story of **the Fisher King**, from the legend of the Holy Grail. This is one of the myths that defines the relationship between **Willard** and Kurtz, and the Grail legend also happily contains a coincidental verbal reference to **Lance**.

The ghostly presence of *The Waste Land* provides a background depth to the action, with the idea that it has been read and understood by the film's authors and characters, that it underlines the literary and mythical lineage of the film, drawing as it does on legend as well as Conrad – it shares and reflects the same, dark, portentous mood.

It also has a more playful role, in my view. **Coppola** has suggested that the film should be appreciated on many different levels, and there is simultaneously a more jokily referential element such as the naming of the **Harrison Ford** character. **John Milius** is apparently incapable of discussing the film without claiming for it some new mythical basis. The presence of *The Waste Land* is part of the film's attempt at self-mythologising. There must be a suggestion that there is a parallel between the poem and the film. *The Waste Land* is a densely referential poem, alluding to, among many others, Dante, Chaucer, Shakespeare, Wagner, Baudelaire, Spenser, Ovid, Homer and Hermann Hesse. The *Apocalypse Now* trainspotter, the anorak semiotician, is, I guess, tempted into treating the film in the same way, continually reviewing it in the quest for hidden clues to deeper meanings.

end, the

This has always been one of the main ingredients in the myth of *Apocalypse Now*. **Coppola** openly admitted that he did not know how to end the film.

What were his options? There was the idea in **John Milius**'s original script, in which **Willard** and **Kurtz** join forces to engage the **Viet Cong** in a climactic battle, and Kurtz shoots down the **helicopter** that comes to rescue them. There is a bit of classic Milius fascist fantasy dialogue, which Milius gets to deliver to camera in *Hearts of Darkness: A Filmmaker's Apocalypse*:

KURTZ: We fight for the land that's under our feet, gold that's in our hands, women that worship the power in our loins. I summon fire from the sky. Do you know what it means to be a white man who can summon fire from the sky? What it means? You can live or die for these things. Not silly ideas that are always betrayed . . . What do you fight for, Captain?

WILLARD: Because it feels good.

Hmmm. This would probably sound OK in a *Conan* film, and in fact the final exchange made it as far as the **French plantation** scene. Coppola wisely decided to discard this ending, meld Milius's vision with **Conrad**'s and add his own inspirations on the shoot. What remained were (with Willard's assassination of Kurtz as a given):

1 Willard remaining in the **jungle** as Kurtz's successor.
2 Willard leaving and calling in the **air strike**.
3 An idea Coppola briefly toyed with – of having Willard double-crossed and being killed in the air strike that he orders – was never filmed.

The 35mm version of the film released in Great Britain ends with the final credits rolling over a scene of Kurtz's **temple** being destroyed by an air strike. This was an extremely expensive sequence and this is one area in which the mythology of the making of the film has entered the consciousness of the audience (or at least its more dedicated members). What emerged as the appropriate and now standard ending *the* ending is the one in which Coppola returned to *Heart of Darkness*:

Marlow ceased, and sat apart, indistinct and silent, in the pose
of a meditating Buddha. Nobody moved for a time. 'We have
lost the first of the ebb,' said the Director, suddenly. I raised my
head. The offing was barred by a black bank of clouds, and the
tranquil waterway leading to the uttermost ends of the earth
flowed sombre under an overcast sky – seemed to lead into the
heart of an immense darkness.

In the film Willard has replaced Kurtz as the **Montagnards'** god; he
walks through them clutching Kurtz's memoirs, collects **Lance** and
together they head off down river. Willard turns off the radio, thus
at least postponing the air strike, and, after a shimmering ghost-like
appearance of a helicopter, flames and a pagan idol juxtaposed with
Willard's camouflaged face, Kurtz's death whisper **'The horror!
The horror!'** is repeated and with the sound of heavy rain (early
screenings of the film had jungle noises piped into the auditorium
before the film began), fade to black. This ending allows for several
possible interpretations. It very conspicuously echoes **the beginning**,
with the reprise of **'The End'** and several visual clues. On some level
we know that the compound will be destroyed – as in the beginning
this is suggested by the barely visible flames – but we do not see this.
Willard has agreed to become the **caretaker** of Kurtz's memory (he
is presumably going to fulfil his promise and speak to Kurtz's son),
and yet it remains ambiguous whether or not he will obey his
instructions and 'Destroy them all'. Will Willard stay in the army?
We know he doesn't want another mission. They are escaping, but
where to?

As in the whole characterisation of Kurtz in Conrad and the film,
this ambiguity in the ending is both a weakness and an advantage. Just
as it is impossible to present a perfect embodiment of pure darkness
and evil, so it is impossible to provide a perfectly fitting conclusion to
a film that deals with war, madness and evil 'on **forty-seven different
levels**'. The film-makers have both solved and slyly avoided this by

layering the ending as carefully as the beginning, so the audience must interpret, fill in its own ending, even possibly the expensive explosive one that has been excised. What is clear is that the boat seems to be heading into the heart of an immense darkness and the film, like the world, ends not with a bang but with a whimper.

'End, The'

Jim Morrison, self-styled Lizard King, who believed that the soul of a recently dead Indian man entered his own when he was a boy, would probably have approved of his music becoming the **soundtrack** to the climactic, violent pagan ritual. He was a fan of shamanism and no stranger to **drugs**, poetic mysticism and **pretentiousness**; for example:

> Ride the snake
> To the lake
> To the ancient lake

It has been said that *Apocalypse Now* begins with 'The End', but it could be said more fully and accurately that it begins with the beginning of 'The End' and (nearly) ends with the end of 'The End'. It skips the middle section, which builds up to:

> The killer awoke before dawn
> He took a face from the ancient gallery . . .
> . . . and then he came to a door and he looked inside
> 'Father.'
> 'Yes.'
> 'I want to kill you.'
> 'Mother, I want to . . .

The last line apart, this overtly Oedipal fantasy is a fair if brief description of this sequence. The inclusion of the song at **the beginning** and **the end** establishes and reinforces the mystical, paternal bond between **Kurtz** and **Willard**, and suggests that the finale is preordained. The neatness of this, considering **Coppola**'s professed panic at having no conception of how to end his film, either suggests chutzpah or underlines the importance of working with a great editor.

Erebus

The name of the **PBR**. It is mentioned by the unnamed narrator of *Heart of Darkness* as one of the boats that would have travelled, like the *Nellie*, up the Thames. *Brewer's Dictionary of Phrase and Fable* says of Erebus:

> In Greek mythology, the son of Chaos and brother of Night; hence darkness personified. His name was given to the gloomy underground cavern through which the Shades had to walk in their passage to Hades.

> Not Erebus itself were dim enough
> To hide thee from prevention
>   Shakespeare: *Julius Caesar*, II, i

This seems to emphasise the darkness of the PBR's destination and reaffirm the link with *Heart of Darkness*. Also the appearance in *Julius Caesar* is probably not coincidental, as the play is one of the key sources (along with *Heart of Darkness*) of **T. S. Eliot**'s **The Hollow Men**, part of which **Kurtz** recites to **Willard**.

Erebus is mentioned in Book IV of Virgil's *The Aeneid*:

> But I should call upon the earth to gape
> and close above me, or on the almighty
> Father to take his thunderbolt, to hurl

me down to the shades, the pallid shadows
and deepest night of Erebus, before
I'd violate you, Shame, or break your laws!

The Aeneid supplied the title for **The Golden Bough**, which is one of
the volumes in **Kurtz's library**.

Escoffier, Georges Auguste (1847–1935)

'King of chefs and chef of kings' born at Villeneuve-Loubet, in
the Alpes Maritimes. He began working in a kitchen aged 12 and
worked in London from 1890 to his retirement in 1921, first at
the Savoy and then the Carlton, where in 1914 he promoted **Ho
Chi Minh**, then known as Nguyen Tat Thanh, to assistant pastry
cook. In *Apocalypse Now* **Chef** was about to complete his training
as a **saucier** at the Escoffier school in Paris when he was drafted.
Students of culinary/film history have not yet reached a consensus
over whether this is meaningful, coincidental or perhaps a meaningful
coincidence.

F

Family, the

Followers of **Charles Manson**, whose exploits are shown in a press cutting sent in a letter to **Chef**, delivered at **Do Long bridge**. A link between Manson and **Kurtz** is suggested by **the photojournalist** referring to Kurtz's **Montagnard** followers as all being 'his children.'

Faust

The volume of **Goethe** seen fleetingly in **Kurtz's library** is presumably *Faust*. While there is no overt reference to the play in *Apocalypse Now*, it suggests and emphasises by its presence elements in the film of themes shared by both – of yearning for experience, perverted utopianism, temptation, evil and an exploration of mythology.

Fishburne, Larry (Laurence) (b. 1961)

He plays **Clean, Mr Clean**, Bubba, Gunner's Mate 3rd Class. The interruption by **Kilgore** when he and **Lance** are first introduced to him prevents the audience from finding out his name. He was only 14 when he was cast in the film. Born in Augusta, Georgia, he was 2 when his family moved to New York City. He made his acting debut off-Broadway aged 10. The prolonged location shoot must have been a strange, disturbing, alien place for a 15-year-old. Although at the time of the film's release it was declared that he

'endured the many hardships of 14 months of **Philippine** location shooting with an ease that was the envy of many older
cast and crew members', Fishburne has since suggested that this
was an illusion. In fact the experience seems to have affected
him almost as profoundly as it did the **Coppolas** and **Martin
Sheen**. Speaking to Andrew Billen, in the *Evening Standard*, he
said:

> My journey into darkness started when I began on *Apoca-
> lypse Now* and I think I started to emerge into the light
> when I was about 27. It was a long journey. But here I
> sit before you, brother, an emissary of the light. Truly. But
> I have experienced great darkness [The effects of the experience
> manifested themselves on his return] . . . in all kinds of ways:
> being irresponsible, being very pessimistic about things, nothing
> was ever good enough – 'I hate everybody,' that kind of
> attitude.

His emergence from the darkness enabled, or was enabled by, the
renewal of his acting career. He took leading roles or strong supporting
ones in *King of New York*, *Boyz N The Hood* and *Deep Cover*, and
seems at last to have established himself as a star playing the title role
opposite Kenneth Branagh's Iago in *Othello* and the main character
in the big-budget *Event Horizon*.

Fisher King, the

I sat upon the shore
Fishing, with the arid plains behind me
Shall I at least set my lands in order?

These lines from **T. S. Eliot**'s *The Waste Land*, as Eliot explains
in his own notes, are inspired by the Fisher King chapter from

Jessie L. Weston's *From Ritual to Romance*, a key influence on Eliot's beliefs in general and this poem in particular, and one of the books in **Kurtz's library**. The Fisher King is one of the figures in the Grail legend, prominent in *The Golden Bough* and central to *From Ritual to Romance*. The latter traces the variations on the character in literature and Christian, pre-Christian, Buddhist and Hindu religions and mythology. What emerges is a complex idea, a character that differs from version to version. *Brewer's Dictionary of Phrase and Fable* describes him simply thus: 'In the legends of the Holy Grail, the uncle of Perceval.' The *Bloomsbury Guide to English Literature*'s entry reads:

> Title of the Grail Keeper in Arthurian legendary narrative. The name first appeared in Chrétien de Troyes' romance *Perceval*, where it is not explained, and is given a Christian interpretation in Robert de Boron's late 12th/early 13th century version of the Grail story. In versions of the 'Quest of the Holy Grail' narrative, the Fisher King is not always the same as the Grail King.

Jessie L. Weston concludes her chapter by acknowledging the difficulties of assimilating the different versions of the character:

> Can it be denied that, while from the standpoint of a Christian interpretation the character of the Fisher King is simply incomprehensible, from the standpoint of the Folk-tale inadequately explained, from that of a ritual survival it assumes a profound meaning and significance? He is not merely a deeply symbolic figure, but the essential centre of the whole cult, a being semi-divine, semi-human, standing between his people and land, and the unseen forces which control their destiny. If the Grail story be based on a Life ritual the character of the Fisher King is of the very essence of the tale, and his title, so

far from being meaningless, expresses, for those who are at pains to seek, the object of the perplexing whole.

This character – the whole myth of the Fisher King and his place within the larger Grail myth, which as *From Ritual to Romance* suggests spreads in various forms across the mythology of disparate cultures – has often been cited as the defining myth of *Apocalypse Now*, certainly symbolic of **Kurtz**'s character and his relationship with **Willard**. We are invited to draw parallels, to seek different interpretations and instantly place the film in a tradition of literature, art and mythology. To distil the Fisher King from his many disparate parts and his function as a reference point for the film, he is a crucial, possibly wounded, figure in a quest. Perhaps the guardian of what is being sought, he is closely linked with water and vegetation rituals, and awaits the arrival of the Knight. The Knight, whose search involves a lance and a vessel (perhaps I'm taking this too far), confronts the Fisher King. The whole myth revolves around the theme of death and regeneration. B. C. Southam, in his *Student's Guide to the Selected Poems of T. S. Eliot*, sums the myth up more succinctly, describing the Fisher King as:

> a figure which recurs in a number of fertility myths. . . . His land is under a curse and laid waste. The Fisher King is impotent, by illness or maiming; and his people are likewise infertile. The curse can only be lifted by the arrival of a stranger who must put or answer certain ritual questions.

This is of course strongly suggestive of the way Willard comes to the compound, speaks to Kurtz, kills him in a ritual slaughter, and leaves with Kurtz's men laying down their **weapons**. **Dennis Jakob**, creative consultant on the film and friend from UCLA Film School days of both **Coppola** and Jim Morrison, introduced the Fisher King concept to the script.

Five-hour version

Near-mythical version of *Apocalypse Now*, featuring for the first half, largely insignificant out-takes, e.g. after the **napalm** speech the **PBR** crew stealling **Kilgore**'s surfboard. It also includes the second meeting with the **Playboy Bunnies** and the whole of the **Clean** funeral/-**French plantation** sequence. Most of the extra material appears in extended scenes with **Willard**, **Kurtz, the photo-journalist** and **Colby**. The idea of this lost footage is appealing but will retain its mystique only as long as it remains unseen.

fog

Fog is a pervasive presence in the film, along with smoke from fires, guns and flares, as it is in ***Heart of Darkness***. It is used as a device to separate the episodes and enhances the dreamlike quality of the action. It was also expensive, as the production used thousands of smoke canisters costing $25 each.

Ford, Harrison (b. 1942)

Actor born in Chicago. He studied English and philosophy at Ripon College, Wisconsin, but did not graduate. He acted in films and on TV from the mid-1960s, but failed to establish himself and worked as much in his fallback profession of carpentry as acting. He was tempted out of retirement to play the out-of-town racer Bob Falfa in *American Graffiti*, which was directed by **George Lucas** and produced by **Francis Coppola**. He had another cameo role as **Robert Duvall**'s assistant in *The Conversation*, before establishing himself as a star as Han Solo in the ***Star Wars*** trilogy and in the *Indiana Jones* trilogy. Meanwhile, he had one more role for Coppola, playing **the Colonel** in the scene where **Willard** receives his mission. He is said to have turned down a larger role, and this may have been a good thing as he acts rather oddly in one of the film's most memorable scenes. It is hard to say whether his sweaty, swallowing, stammering performance is effective or overacting, or even indicative of his discomfort in front of the camera. Still he gets to say Nu Mung Bha and deliver the line 'Now he's crossed into Cambodia with this **Montagnard** army of his that worship the man like a god, and follow every order however ridiculous', with unusual, unsettling emphasis.

Melissa Mathison, the screenwriter of *E.T. – The Extra Terrestrial* and Ford's future wife, worked on the film as an executive assistant. Although the name is (deliberately?) mumbled, **the General** (**G. D. Spradlin**) says to Ford, 'Lucas, would you play that tape to the Captain, please?' His character is jokily called **Colonel G. Lucas**.

See **'Terminate with extreme prejudice'**; **Nha Trang**.

Forrest, Frederic (b. 1936)

Leading/character actor, born Waxahachie, Texas. He studied drama under the hugely influential Sanford Meisner and Lee Strasberg before performing off-Broadway. His early promise was acknowledged with a Golden Globe nomination for Best New-comer for his role in *When the Legends Die*, and he continued strongly in **Coppola**'s *The Conversation*, in which he and Cindy Williams were the couple whose tryst was taped. Towards the end of the 1970s and beginning of the 1980s the stature of his roles peaked with *The Missouri Breaks*, *Apocalypse Now* and *The Rose*. The consecutive conspicuous failures of *One From the Heart* and *Hammett* seemed to mark the end of his time as a leading player, and he settled smoothly into a career as a reliably eccentric character actor. Among his notable films are Coppola's *Tucker: The Man and His Dream*, *Music Box*, *The Two Jakes* and *Falling Down*, in which he comes over like a louder, more intense, bigoted version of **Chef**.

As Peter Cowie says in *Coppola*, 'Forrest had already appeared in *Viet Rock*, one of the earliest off-Broadway plays about the war. "I'd lived in New York in the 1960s," Forrest says, "so I wanted to make an anti-war statement in *Apocalypse*."' With his excellent, tightly wound performance as **Hicks**, 'Chef', the **saucier**, he has the authenticity and depth common to all aspects of the production. Like the other actors, he seems either to have been perfectly chosen or to have adopted the characteristics of his on-screen persona. Chef is explicitly out of place in **Vietnam**; he is someone who should be in a kitchen preparing sauces. He is, almost as much as **Willard**, the eyes through which the action is seen, and where Willard is focused and impassive, Chef is constantly on the edge of hysteria. He can't cope with the war, the **tiger**, the **sampan** attack; it is he who points out to Willard (in case he hadn't noticed) that what **Kurtz** has going is 'fuckin' pagan idolatry'. Tellingly, in ***Hearts of Darkness: A Filmmaker's Apocalypse***, Frederic Forrest recalls feeling the same way, wanting to get out but knowing that he couldn't leave, so fantasising an escape.

> It was crazy, you know, slightly mad. The whole thing was mad, you know. We felt like, after a while, we really weren't there. It was like you were in a dream or something. We would say to Francis, 'I'm not here, Francis. I'm in Montana with **Jack Nicholson**.' So they'd say, 'Where are you today, Freddie?' And I'd be in Waco, I could be in Des Moines, wherever I wanted to be. And you could just go through your day, and you weren't in that place.

See **decapitation**; **'Never get out of the boat'**.

forty-seven different levels

Asked about the different levels of meaning in the film, **Walter Murch** says:

> It's one of the characteristics of the film. It certainly kept us going. The more we dug into it, the more it resonated on all these different levels. When you got it down to the third

or fourth level, you'd suddenly see, maybe we could get this fifth level. Whenever you're making a film, that's what keeps you alive and ticking. Even though you think no audience will get this, it keeps me interested in doing it. I guess it's what a painter would do with a little bit of detail in the background of a painting, thinking that colour resonates with this. The audience picks it up on an intuitive visceral level.

In *Hearts of Darkness: A Filmmaker's Apocalypse* **Coppola** explains:

Nothing is so terrible as a pretentious movie. . . . On one hand trying to aspire to really do something, and on the other, you're just not allowed to be pretentious. Finally you say, Fuck it. I don't care if I'm pretentious or not pretentious. Or if I've done it or I haven't done it. All I know is I'm going to see this movie and for me it has to have some answers. And by answers I don't mean a punch-line, I mean answers on about forty-seven different levels. And it's very difficult to talk about this thing without being very corny. You use a word like 'self-purgation' and 'epiphany', they think you're either a religious weirdo or a college professor. But those are the words for the process. This transmutation, this renaissance, this rebirth, which is the basis for all life. The one rule that all men, from the time they first were walking around, looking at the sun, scratching around for food and an animal to kill, the first concept that I feel got into their head was the idea of life and death, that the sun went down and the sun went up, that the crops. . . . In Winter everything died. . . . The first man must have thought, 'Oh my God, it's the end of the world.' And then, all of a sudden there's Spring and everything's alive and it's better. I mean after all, look at **Vietnam**, look at my movie. You'll see what I'm talking about.

This is both explanation and tease. With this the viewer is encouraged to look for different meanings and interpretations within the film, though not literally on forty-seven levels, you guess. The particular significance referred to here is the film's loaded climax, establishing its mythical lineage to ancient ideas and stories of rebirth and primitive vegetation rituals via **T. S. Eliot, *From Ritual to Romance* and *The Golden Bough*.** Interestingly, Coppola, interviewed here on the film's location, intended a more definite, less ambiguous – if not quite optimistic – ending than the one that emerged during the **editing** process.

Frazer, Sir James George (1854–1941)

Scottish classical scholar, translator and anthropologist who produced many translations (including Ovid's verse), and wrote, among others, *Totemism* and *Folk-lore in the Old Testament*. His most famous work remains the seminal study in comparative religion *The Golden Bough*, which is one of the few volumes seen on **Kurtz**'s reading table.

Frederickson, Gray

One of the film's co-producers. He has worked for **Coppola** in various production roles, often with **Fred Roos**, from *The Godfather* onwards and has enjoyed a good working relationship with him. The notable exception was during the shoot for *One From the Heart*, when a furious Coppola hurled costly china plates at him. As Peter Cowie recalls in *Coppola*, 'Frederickson ducked most of them.'

French plantation

In **Heart of Darkness Marlow** says, 'Going up that river was like travelling back to the earliest beginnings of the world, when vegetation rioted on the earth and the big trees were kings.' This image of travelling up river as a journey back through time was adapted into the story of *Apocalypse Now*. **Coppola** has said:

My idea was that as they progressed up the river, they were going back more and more in time in a funny kind of way.

That we were revisiting the history of **Vietnam** in reverse and
the first stop was in the '50s almost. We now are with the French,
that was what I was looking for in the French plantation. That
it was a kind of ghostly afterview of something, almost like
they talk about the light from stars. We see it after the star's
already dead.

This sequence is one of those that is present in the mysterious
five-hour version but was wholly removed from the final cut.
The host tries to explain how the French attitude and relationship to
Vietnam differs crucially from the American. In ***Hearts of Darkness: A***
***Filmmaker's Apocalypse* Milius** renders it thus: 'If they drive us from
our house, we will live in a ditch, if they push us out of the ditch, we
will live in the **jungle**. All the time we will clean the blood from
our bayonets' (authentic Milius-style speech). The plantation-owner
concludes, 'You are American. You are fighting for the biggest piece
of nothing in history' (surely not Milius).

The sequence ends with **Willard** and a French woman sharing an
after-dinner cognac, then opium and finally a candle-lit canopy bed.
Their goofed post-coital chat concludes with an exchange borrowed
from Milius's ditched original ending dialogue between **Kurtz** and
Willard. She asks him, 'Why do you fight?' He replies, 'Because
I like it.'

Coppola wanted the ghostliness of the sequence to be enhanced by
having everything seen through wisps of smoke, the interiors apparently lit only by the natural candlelight. Everything was organised with
meticulous attention to authentic detail. Coppola specified that:

White wine should be served ice cold. Red wine should be
served at 58 degrees, should be opened approximately an hour
to an hour-and-a-half to even two hours before serving. I want
a French ceremony that is right out of . . . I want the French to
say, 'My God! How did they do that?'

As it turned out, the scene was beautifully designed, decorated and lit, but the same care was impossible for the casting. Coppola says that he was unable to get the actors he wanted for the sequence and so hated it and dumped it. This is presumably largely true, but can't tell the whole story. In a sense the episode seems a little misconceived and **pretentious**. The idea of the journey back through time is neat and is suggested in the film as it stands, with the river becoming increasingly primeval and the boat and the crew being gradually consumed by the river and the jungle. But everything is too much on the surface here. Where elsewhere in the film there are suggestions and symbols (however obvious or crude), the audience can decide for itself what to make of the war, of **colonialism** and imperialism, of **drugs** and killing. Here it seems it was considered necessary to introduce a history lesson, to have literal representatives of Vietnam's colonised past.

Richard Marks points out that the cutting of this sequence denies **Clean** his funeral:

> The audience has started to identify with Clean, so part of the reason for the French Rubber Plantation sequence was to have them getting off the boat and asking permission to bury him on their land. You had a full military funeral. This whole episode was truly a magnificently ambitious sequence, but it stopped the narrative flow. It would have been perfect, but it stopped the film dead.

It is a shame that no vestige of this sequence remains in the finished film, except – and this is pushing it – as ghostly traces for those in the audience who know that it exists in some file somewhere, have seen extracts from it in *Hearts of Darkness* and in magazine articles (if not the actual scenes themselves in illicit copies of the five-hour version), and can imagine it as more mysterious, profound, and better acted and written than it actually is.

From Ritual to Romance

Published in 1920, and partly inspired by **J. G. Frazer**'s *The Golden Bough*, **Jessie L. Weston**'s scholarly work is one of the volumes seen among **Kurtz**'s belongings. It examines the myth of the Grail, holy and otherwise. The author traces the myth from its relatively modern versions as a quest for a Christian relic, back to its origins as a Gnostic story, and investigates the pervasive sexual symbolism of the Lance and the Grail and the character of **the Fisher King**, who features (in different incarnations) in many of the versions. The legend of the Fisher King, as a story of a beleaguered man, his people and land awaiting regeneration brought by a visiting stranger on a quest, is consciously suggestive of the film's climax (and ultimate meaning?) and the figure of the lance is represented by, er, **Lance**.

See **Eliot, T. S.**

G

gardenias

Kurtz, discovering that **Willard** is from Ohio, reminisces about a childhood journey down the **Ohio river**, when he came upon what must once have been a gardenia plantation: 'For about five miles you'd think that heaven had fallen to earth in the form of gardenias.' This is presumably partly a memory from **Brando**'s own childhood, although **John Milius** says:

> I remember a speech that I wrote about the scent of gardenias coming in from the shore to the **jungle**, but I think the finished speech came from Brando.

Gauguin, Paul (1848–1903)

French artist of the post-Impressionist school. He started out as stockbroker and patron of several early Impressionist painters before becoming a professional painter himself. Like **Marlon Brando**, he fell in love with and settled in the South Seas, marrying a local woman and having several lovers. **Coppola** suggested to Brando that he use him as a model for his conception of the role of **Kurtz** as someone who 'went native'.

General, the

In the scene in **Nha Trang** where **Willard** receives his orders the anonymous General delivers one of the film's most powerful, menacing speeches:

You see, Willard, in this war things get confused – power,
ideals, your own morality, practical military necessity. But out
there with these natives there must be a temptation to be God.
Because there's a conflict in every human heart between the
rational and the irrational, between good and evil, and good
does *not* always triumph. Sometimes the dark side overcomes
what Lincoln called 'the better angels of our nature.' Every man
has got a breaking point – you and I have. Walter **Kurtz** has
reached his and very obviously he has gone insane.

In this speech, three times he invokes the spirit of **Conrad**. The idea of
the temptation to be God echoes one of the three brief extracts quoted
from Kurtz's report to the International Society for the Repression of
Savage Customs. As **Marlow** recalls it:

'He began with the argument that we whites, from the point
of development we had arrived at, "must necessarily appear
to them [savages] in the nature of supernatural beings – we
approach them with the might as of a deity."'

When Marlow sees what Kurtz has done he observes: 'Evidently the
appetite for more ivory had got the better of the – what shall I say –
less material aspirations.'

Finally, there is the echo of Marlow's observation that Kurtz's soul
was mad: 'Being alone in the wilderness, it had looked within itself,
and, by heavens! I tell you, it had gone mad.'

The General concludes that Kurtz is 'out there operating without
any decent restraint, totally beyond the pale of any acceptable human
conduct and he is still in the field commanding troops'. The notion
of 'restraint' is a theme of *Heart of Darkness*. Marlow admires the
cannibals for not eating their companions: 'Restraint! What possible
restraint? . . . And these chaps had no earthly reason for any kind of

scruple. Restraint, I would have just as soon expected restraint from a hyena prowling amongst the corpses of a battlefield.'

Talking of the dead helmsman, Marlow says, 'Poor fool! If he had only left the shutter alone. He had no restraint, no restraint – just like Kurtz – a tree swayed by the wind.' On seeing the impaled heads at the Inner Station he notes that 'Mr Kurtz lacked restraint in the gratification of his various lusts'.

The General is played by the instantly sinister **G. D. Spradlin**. You can't help but associate him with his previous role for **Coppola** – the devious, hypocritical Senator in *The Godfather Part II*. In that film he first appears to be a friend of the Corleones, making a sycophantic speech at Michael's son's lavish confirmation party in the opening scene. Behind closed doors he is shown to be contemptuous of them. Big mistake. He is last seen weeping, apparently suffering from temporary amnesia, with his trousers down, sitting next to a brutally murdered prostitute, with, naturally, Tom Hagen to help him out. This is a variation of the surprise horse's head/**Chef**'s head theme – perhaps a *leitmotif* in the Coppola *oeuvre*.

This is efficient type-casting of Spradlin, as he plays another authority figure beneath whose cool, sophisticated demeanour and practised eloquence lies danger. You immediately know him to be capable of violence and betrayal. The character is secretly and playfully named after Coppola's mentor, Roger Corman.

Glenn, (Theodore) Scott (b. 1942)

The actor who plays **Colby**. He was born in Pittsburgh, Pennsylvania. After attending William and Mary College in Virginia, a spell in the marines and an early career in journalism, he headed to New York to study acting. Apart from his debut in *The Baby Maker* and his role as a psychotic soldier in *Nashville* (which must have helped him land the role as the psychotic soldier in *Apocalypse Now*), his films were largely unworthy of his talents. He has since lent his wiry presence to such films as *The Right Stuff*, *Silverado* and *The Silence of the Lambs*. His career ought to have been given an early boost by *Apocalypse*, but unfortunately his role was reduced in **editing** to an enigmatic mute cameo.

See **camouflage**; **five-hour version**.

Gods Country

Nickname of **Lance**'s gun on the **PBR**.

See **Canned Heat**.

Goethe, Johann Wolfgang von (1749–1832)

German poet, philosopher, playwright and novelist.

See *Faust*.

Golden Bough, The

Subtitled *A Study in Magic and Religion* and published in twelve volumes between 1890 and 1915; the one-volume version shown in **Kurtz**'s room is probably the abridgement, edited by the author **Sir James Frazer** and his wife, Lilly, which appeared in 1922. The book is relevant to the film in several ways. Firstly, it is significant in terms of its subject matter. It is a comprehensive if controversial work of comparative religion that contains a lengthy chapter in its abridged form entitled 'Killing the God', which examines at length many different forms of ritual slaughter, and how these are used to appease and revive deities. Second, it became a seminal work that fed into twentieth-century mysticism and theology, influencing, among others, two writers whose work features in **Kurtz's library**, **T. S. Eliot** and **Jessie L. Weston**. Lastly, there is the title itself, which comes from Book VI of Virgil's *Aeneid*, which **John Milius** has cited as a key influence on the film. After the destruction of Troy and on the mission to found Rome, Aeneas' father Anchises dies. Wanting to visit him one last time in the Underworld, Aeneas consults the Sybil at Cumae, who gives him instructions on how to gain entrance to the Underworld; these include the following (from William Pitt's translation):

> A mighty tree that bears a golden bough,
> Grows in a vale surrounded by a grove,
> And sacred to the queen of Stygian Jove.
> Her nether world no mortals can behold,
> Till from the bole they strip the blooming gold.

gooks

Another slang term for the Vietnamese. **Kilgore** complains laughingly about how all the 'gook names sound the same'. Its use as a perjorative name for East Asians of any nationality dates back at least as far as the 1920s.

See **racism**.

Graham, Angelo

Art director. Frequent collaborator of **Coppola**'s from *The Godfather Part II* onwards, usually in tandem with production designer **Dean Tavoularis**.

Graham, Bill

Rock music impresario who plays **Playboy Bunnies**' agent in an apparent impersonation of **Richard Nixon**. After the shoot he invited **Francis** and **Eleanor Coppola** to a Grateful Dead concert which inspired Coppola to form the band **the Rhythm Devils**, who play some of the **soundtrack** music. Ironically, Graham died in a **helicopter** crash.

Green Berets

The Special Forces group that **Kurtz** finally managed to join at his third attempt. As **Willard** says, 'Thirty-eight years old. Why the fuck would he do that?' In **John Milius**'s original draft Willard joined Kurtz's band of renegade Green Berets in a climactic battle against the **Viet Cong**. The film emphasises the splintered nature of the American military machine, with the regular army, Navy, **Air Cavalry** and Marines either actively hostile to one another or co-operating only reluctantly. This reflects the reality of the war as described by **Michael Herr** in *Dispatches*, which is full of stories of the open contempt between the Army and the Marines. Kurtz's desire to join the Green Berets suggests his disillusionment with the inefficiency and hypocrisy of the official war effort, and his efforts to be more independent and ruthless. Herr recalls seeing a sign in a Special Forces camp in **Vietnam** that read: 'IF YOU KILL FOR MONEY YOU'RE A MERCENARY. IF YOU KILL FOR PLEASURE YOU'RE A SADIST. IF YOU KILL FOR BOTH YOU'RE A GREEN BERET.' The Green Berets were in the vanguard of US military involvement in South-east Asia, active in Vietnam, Laos and Cambodia from 1957 onwards.

Gregory, Paul

Military adviser on the project who spoke local **Philippine** dialects and headed security operations.

H

Hackman, Gene (b. 1930)

Character actor who became a leading man in the early 1970s, after winning the Best Actor Oscar for his performance as Popeye Doyle in *The French Connection*. He is brilliant as the obsessive surveillance man/sound expert Harry Caul in **Coppola**'s *The Conversation* and was Coppola's original choice for the role of **Kilgore**.

Hall, Albert (b. 1937)

Sometimes Albert P. Hall, possibly to distinguish himself from the London auditorium and to avoid being continually referred to as a solidly built actor. In *Apocalypse Now* he played Chief. In films he has largely acted in supporting roles. He appeared in several New York Shakespeare Festival plays, off-Broadway and Broadway productions and featured, along with **Larry Fishburne**, in an ABC-TV special *If You Give a Dance, You Gotta Pay the Band*. His other films include *Cotton Comes to Harlem*, *Shamus*, *Willie Dynamite* and *Leadbelly*. Since *Apocalypse Now* he has appeared in *The Fabulous Baker Boys*, *The Music Box*, *Malcolm X* and *Devil in a Blue Dress*.

Hard in Darkness

See **'In the Nam of the Father'**.

Hau Phat

The **Philippine** location for the United Services Overseas **Playboy Bunnies** sequence.

heads

In **Conrad**'s *Heart of Darkness* as the steamboat approaches the Inner Station **Marlow** observes the compound:

> 'There was no enclosure or fence of any kind, but there had been one apparently, for near the house half a dozen slim posts remained in a row, roughly trimmed, and with their upper ends ornamented with round carved balls.'

As he gets closer, he observes:

> 'And then I made a brusque movement and one of the remaining posts of that vanished fence leaped up in the field of my glass. You remember I told you I had been struck at the distance by certain attempts at ornamentation, rather remarkable in the ruinous aspect of the place. Now I had suddenly a nearer view and its first result was to make me throw my head back as if before a blow. These round knobs were not ornamental but symbolic; symbolic of some cruel and forbidden knowledge. They were expressive and puzzling, striking and disturbing – food for thought and also for vultures if there had been any looking down from the sky; but at all events for such ants as were industrious enough to ascend the pole. They would have been more impressive, those heads on the stakes, if their faces had not been turned to the house. Only one, the first I had made out, was facing my way ... there was nothing exactly

profitable in these heads being there. They only showed that Mr **Kurtz** lacked restraint in the gratification of his various lusts, that there was something wanting in him – some small matter which when the pressing need arose could not be found under his magnificent eloquence. Whether he knew of this deficiency himself I can't say. I think the knowledge came to him at last – only at the very last . . . .

'The admirer of Mr Kurtz was a bit crestfallen. In a hurried, indistinct voice he began to assure me he had not dared to take these – say, symbols – down.'

In *Apocalypse Now* when **the photo-journalist** sees **Willard** looking around at the heads strewn all over the steps leading to the ruined **temple** he sighs, as if excusing a small misdemeanour: 'The heads, the heads. You're looking at the heads. Sometimes he goes too far – he's the first to admit it.' This line, like **Hopper**'s entire performance, provides some strange light relief but – and this may be pedantic – marks a shift from *Heart of Darkness*, so Kurtz's last words signify less of a sudden, final self-realisation.

The extras playing the heads had to endure days of shooting while buried up to their necks. In breaks in the filming they were sheltered by parasols and given drinks, so supplying one of the more memorably bizarre scene in *Hearts of Darkness: A Filmmaker's Apocalypse*. The presence of disembodied heads also probably explains the quotation from *If–* and so, also, the dubious Kurtzian observation on the hidden semantic properties of the word 'life'.

See **decapitation**.

heart attack

If you know only two things about *Apocalypse Now* they are that **Kilgore** loves the smell of **napalm** in the morning and that **Martin Sheen** suffered a near-fatal heart attack during the strenuous shoot.

The widely reported problems in **the Philippines**, the spiralling cost, destructive weather and, most of all, the near-death of the film's star all seem in retrospect to have been used as effective *ad hoc* marketing. Thus, a film that was designed as a modern myth was granted near-mythical status even in its making, long before anyone had seen it.

The idea that such a project dealing with war, madness and evil should drive an actor close to death clearly added a frisson of excitement and real danger to the film's appeal. This was scary method acting. Coppola consciously presents himself as a kind of tyrant as well as a showman – he has described the film director as the last dictatorial post remaining. Although presumably concerned for Martin Sheen as a person as well as an asset, his reaction to this crisis was similar to that towards the elemental disasters during the shoot. He was frustrated that he couldn't control everything. What really seems to have scared him was the 'gossip', the fact that his personal assistant **Melissa Mathison** had spoken to the studio before clearing it with him. He said, 'If Marty dies I want to hear that everything's OK until I say that Marty is dead.'

This is usually referred to simply as a heart attack, although, tellingly, in *Hearts of Darkness: A Filmmaker's Apocalypse*, **Sam Bottoms** describes it as a breakdown. Sheen was smoking up to sixty cigarettes a day, drinking heavily, working intensively, appearing in virtually every scene, and suffering from nightmares and mental exhaustion. On 5 March 1977 he awoke 'feeling like there was a red hot poker' on his chest. He appears to have suffered a simultaneous heart attack and nervous breakdown. He crawled from his hotel room to the side of the road, where he was spotted by the driver of the production's wardrobe van. He was rushed to an office where he confessed his sins to and was given the last rites by a Filipino priest who understood and spoke no English. From there he was taken by helicopter to the intensive care unit of a Manila hospital, where for the next six weeks he received physical treatment while his wife Janet arranged for psychotherapy by telephone from a therapist in New York City.

Sheen has explained that during the night of the attack he knew that he was close to death and that he himself had the choice of whether he would live or die. During Sheen's lay-off **Coppola** continued shooting around Sheen, using Sheen's brother as a stand-in, who was filmed from behind, and filming the **air strike** destruction of **Kurtz**'s compound. At one stage a part of the **temple** collapsed on to where Coppola would have been standing if he hadn't postponed the scene. Then in a combination of extraordinary psychosomatic empathy for Martin Sheen and **Willard** and exhaustion, Coppola collapsed and himself had a near-death experience complete with 'reality receding down a dark tunnel'. Martin Sheen returned to the set apparently fully recovered on 19 April 1977.

Heart of Darkness

Long short story/short novel by **Joseph Conrad**, published in 1902. **Charlie Marlow** recounts his tale to an anonymous narrator, the Director of Companies, the Lawyer and the Accountant as they sit aboard the cruising yawl the *Nellie* and wait for the tide to turn. His aunt has helped him gain employment from **the Company** to captain a steamboat on an unnamed river in an unnamed country (clearly the Congo in the Belgian Congo). At the Company's Outer Station the elegantly turned-out chief accountant appears in stark contrast to the natives, who are sick and starving.

When he arrives at the Central Station he finds that his progress is halted for several months as his ship is half-submerged. Marlow begins to hear more and more rumours and reports of **Kurtz**, the company's finest agent, a prodigious supplier of ivory and generally a remarkable man. Finally the steamboat departs with Marlow, several Company representatives and a crew of cannibals. As they near the Inner Station, of which Kurtz is the agent, they suffer an attack by tiny **arrows** which ends with the helmsman being killed by a **spear**. They are greeted at the station by an eccentric Russian trader and the sight of Kurtz's quarters surrounded by impaled **heads**. From his encounters with Kurtz and the report for the International Society for The Suppression of Savage Customs, which Marlow read on the journey, Marlow finds Kurtz to be a gifted, eloquent man whose methods have become suspect. He is also very sick, and is relieved of his posting and transported down river on Marlow's steamboat. His condition deteriorates, and one evening he quietly cries before dying: **'The horror! The horror!'**

Marlow retreats from the edge of madness and savagery, over which Kurtz had stepped, and returns to England, where over a year later he visits Kurtz's fiancée. He tells her that Kurtz's last utterance was her name. With that, Marlow's account ends and the five men sit on the boat under an overcast sky.

This is a remarkable story that combines rich, overwrought descriptive language with a frustrating, deliberate opacity. We know that Kurtz is a remarkable, eloquent and ultimately mad man, but learn little of his actions and read almost none of his written or spoken words. The occasional vagueness of Conrad's narrative and a particular obfuscation in his characterisation of Kurtz has several times been criticised by, among others, the literary critic F. R. Leavis. *Apocalypse Now* has been similarly attacked, and in both cases the criticism seems to miss the point. Both book and film use indefiniteness consciously; in the presentation of madness and evil, both ultimately rely as much on suggestion as on simple depiction.

Apocalypse Now is of course not a film version of the novella. *Heart of Darkness* is one of the main inspirations behind the film, but it has been fused with the **Vietnam** experience, the vision and imagination of the film's creators (**Francis Coppola**, **John Milius**, **Michael Herr**, **Vittorio Storaro**, **Walter Murch**, **Richard Marks**, **Dennis Jakob**, *et al.*), and a wider literary and mythical tradition. However, it does remain of vital importance to the film's tone and content. The specific influences are mentioned throughout this guide, and they extend from the central themes of the corruption inherent in colonial exploitation, to the scenario of a remarkably gifted and efficient representative of this power rejecting this hypocrisy and establishing himself as a maverick god-like figure way upriver, deep in the **jungle**. The film adopts the book's central plot structure of an experienced captain being engaged to check Kurtz's activities and becoming increasingly obsessed with Kurtz on his journey up river.

Several incidents are transposed from book to film relatively unchanged; some of the language and characters are also shared. Both the book and film are filled with smoke and **fog**, and continually use images of light and darkness to emphasise their characters' struggle.

Heart of Darkness was adapted by Orson Welles as a radio production for his Mercury Company and it was also to have been his first film when he went to Hollywood in late 1939. As John Houseman, who collaborated with Welles in his early career, says in his memoirs, *Unfinished Business*, the radio production had been only a 'moderate success', but he thought Welles was attracted to return to this source material by the 'sense of corroding evil, the slow, pervasive deterioration through which the dark continent destroys its conqueror and exploiter, Western Man, in the person of Kurtz'. Welles arrived in Hollywood filled with enthusiasm and ambition. He planned to direct and play both Marlow and Kurtz, and intended to use a subjective camera throughout, with the audience (after a direct explanation of the device by Welles himself, spoken over a montage of images including a golfer and a man going to the electric chair) seeing the whole film as if through Marlow's eyes.

More pertinently to *Apocalypse Now*, Welles's script transposed the action to South America, updated it to the present day and presented Kurtz as a modern fascist, explicitly likened to Hitler. However, the project was thwarted by insoluble problems with the script, casting and budget, including Welles's insistence on the employment of

3,000 'very black' extras. Instead, his first film was *Citizen Kane*, another study of a mad, hollow genius who, as Simon Callow points out in *The Road to Xanadu*, 'dies with a mysterious phrase on his lips'.

The conspicuous failure of Orson Welles to bring the project to the screen was a factor in inspiring John Milius to adapt the novel – it was also a favourite book of his as a young man. But it is a fellow member of the original **Zoetrope** team, Carroll Ballard, who lays claim to being the first to come up with the idea of making a film of *Heart of Darkness*, when he tried to buy the screen rights in 1967.

Hearts of Darkness: A Filmmaker's Apocalypse

Directed by **Fax Bahr** and **George Hickenlooper**. A brilliant documentary about the making of *Apocalypse Now*. **Eleanor Coppola** was engaged to make a film about the production. Twelve years later the footage she shot in rehearsals, on location and in Napa, along with the taped conversations of her and **Francis Coppola** and recent interview material with many of the key players (**Sheen**, **Duvall**, **Hopper**, **Hall**, **Bottoms**, **Forrest**, **Fishburne**, as well as the producers and the Coppolas themselves), provides many insights and revelations about how triumph emerged from apparent chaos. The documentary features many scenes from the film, including the **Saigon** hotel room sequence, the dawn raid and **napalm** speech, the **tiger**, the **Playboy Bunnies**, the **sampan**, the **arrows**, **Kurtz**'s **temple** and the **sacrifice**/assassination. These are often skilfully juxtaposed with documentary footage, so that, among other things, you see the odd sight of Coppola and the crew lobbing the tiny arrows on to the **PBR**.

There are also out-takes and scenes that were cut from the release print. These include shots from the hotel scene when Martin Sheen is drunkenly cursing himself and Coppola, having punched the mirror and cut his thumb for real; glimpses of the **French plantation** sequence, the scene around the dinner table in which the Frenchman tells **Willard** that the Americans are fighting for 'the biggest nothing' of all time; a scene of Willard emerging from the boat in the midst of a torrential downpour, presumably in the sequence when they are refuelling before arriving at Kurtz's compound; several out-takes from **Brando**/Kurtz's improvised ramblings, including – memorably – Brando swallowing a bug and being put off by the chattering of an off-screen bird, 'My only critic'.

The film's only narration is supplied by Eleanor Coppola reading extracts from the diary she kept at the time, published in 1979 as *Notes*. Among the film's many highlights (Coppola's assertion that Brando had arrived on the set not having read *Heart of Darkness*, his conversation with Dennis Hopper in which he tries to explain that he can't forget his lines until he has first learnt them, his taped fury at the 'gossip' surrounding Martin Sheen's **heart attack**), it is perhaps **Milius**'s enthusiastic contributions that stand out most starkly. When he recalls being brought back on to the project he says that:

> everybody said, 'Thank God he's returned to reason. . . . This thing will finally be released. Go in there and tell him, tell him he's been crazy.' And I felt like von Rundstedt going to see Hitler in 1944 and I was going to be telling him that there was no more gasoline on the Eastern Front and the whole thing was going to fold. I came out an hour-and-a-half later and he had convinced me that this was going to be the first film that would win a Nobel Prize. So I came out of the room like von Rundstedt, 'We can win. We don't need gasoline.' He had completely turned me around. I would have done anything.

The documentary is an essential companion piece to *Apocalypse Now* – brilliant, outstanding in every way.

helicopters

The film's most famous scene is undoubtedly the **Air Cavalry**'s dawn helicopter raid on the **Viet Cong** village, shown from the perspective of the attackers and the attacked, and accompanied by Richard Wagner's '**The Ride of the Valkyries**'. **Vietnam** is described as the first modern war, and this was demonstrated by the scatter-bombing of B-52s, the **napalm** attacks and the ubiquitous helicopters. The helicopter, which had first been used widely in the Korean War, in an early and relatively clumsy form, became crucial to the ability of the Americans to wage war effectively in Vietnam. This was due to the development of technology and its adaptation as a fighting as well as a transport vehicle. In Korea helicopters designed for light transport were crudely customised as assault vehicles by strapping machine-guns to the sides, which were fired by the pilot or co-pilot pulling wires attached to the trigger.

The modern helicopter became a feature, an essential component, of the **Vietnam War**, used for assault and transport, providing a distinctive sound for the film and the war. The helicopter and its noise haunt the film and **Willard**'s dreams. You are instantly enveloped in the soundscape of the war, by the effect of the sound of the whirring of the fan seguing into that of a circling helicopter.

Neil Sheehan, author of *Bright Shining Lie*, confirms the helicopter as the sight and sound of the Vietnam War: 'I'll hear those blades going whup whup whup whup for the rest of my life.' On location **Coppola**'s personal helicopter pilot, **Dick White**, a Vietnam vet, served as an aerial co-ordinator for the helicopter scenes and narrowly avoided a fatal crash when a stone just missed his helicopter's rear rotor blade. The helicopters used in the dawn raid were hired from **the Philippine** government and several times during the shooting were called away to fight the rebels in the north of the country.

See **Huey, the**.

Hendrix, Jimi

See **'Purple Haze'**.

Herr, Michael

Born in Syracuse, New York. He started out as a film reviewer for *New Leader* magazine. Between 1967 and 1968 he filed several stories for *Esquire* magazine on his experiences and observations of the **Vietnam War**. **'The Battle for Khe Sanh'** was a particular source of material and atmosphere for the film, but in general his pieces were important for the way they conveyed with apparent authenticity and personal ambivalence the chaos, the **drugs** and **rock 'n' roll** of the war. These reports were slowly edited and collated into book form as the remarkable **Dispatches**, published in 1977.

While **Walter Murch** was involved in **editing** the film and organising the **sound** he reintroduced the original notion of the **voice-over**, which **Coppola** had rejected. He simply used the existing narration, which he recorded using his own voice and placed over the action. Coppola, seeing the logic in this idea but realising the inadequacy of the script in that form, decided to bring Herr in. Herr began work on the narration in February 1978. As he explains in Peter Cowie's *Coppola*, 'The narration written thus far was totally useless. So, over a period of a year I wrote various narrations. Francis gave me very close guidelines. It was a new experience for me and, I must say, a great experience.'

Willard's narration is vitally important to the film's impact – it provides powerful commentary on the action, enhances the film's effects and provides several of its more memorable lines. It fits seamlessly with the mood of the film, often echoing and repeating lines spoken – **'Never get out of the boat'**, **'Some day this war's gonna end'** – and spiralling off to invoke images from his own *Dispatches* as well as returning to the film's source, **Heart of Darkness** – 'for my sins', 'a river that snakes through the war', etc.

Since the double impact of *Apocalypse* and *Dispatches*, in the late 1970s, Herr has, among other things, written a novel, collaborated with artist Guy Peellaert to create the informal, poetic history of Las Vegas *The Big Room*, as well as acting as consultant on other **Vietnam** films, including *Full Metal Jacket*, on which he has a script-writing credit with Gustav Hasford and Stanley Kubrick.

Hickenlooper, George

Co-director of documentary, **Hearts of Darkness: A Filmmaker's Apocalypse**.

Hicks

Although it is never used in the release version of the film, this is the surname of **Chef**. The name presumably represents an implicit comment on the fact that the majority of combat troops in **Vietnam** were blacks or hicks.

Ho Chi Minh (1892–1969)

Born in Nghe An province in central **Vietnam**. He was originally named Nguyen Tat Thanh and used numerous pseudonyms and *noms de plume*, including Nguyen Ai Quoc, Mr C. M. Coo, Guy N'Qua, Nguyen Lai, Nam Son, Thau Chin, Tran Luc, Tuyet Lan, Le Thanh Long and Dan Viet. His assumed name means 'he who enlightens'. Born into French colonial Indo-China, he travelled widely in his early adulthood and founded the Indo-Chinese Communist Party in Hong Kong in 1930. He returned to Vietnam after thirty years in

1941, was given the title of respect 'Uncle' and formed the Viet Nam Doc Lap Dong Minh or Vietminh – the League for an Independent Vietnam.

On 25 August 1945 Ho Chi Minh declared Vietnam a Democratic Republic and called for a national resistance war. The conflict over the next nine years between the Vietminh and the French in the first Indo-China War foreshadowed that between the **Viet Cong** and the Americans in the **Vietnam War**. The Vietminh under Ho, as the VC would later, adopted the standard pattern for guerrilla warfare – **assassinations**, hit-and-run raids, booby traps – having withdrawn from the cities and based themselves in the mountains. The French tried to force the Vietminh to engage in conventional warfare, convinced that their superior fire-power and force of numbers would bring victory.

The fall of the French base at Dien Bien Phu on 7 May 1954 marked the end of the war, the defeat of the French and the end of their colonial power. The division of Vietnam was fragile, and the stand-off between the North Vietnamese communists under Ho and the South Vietnamese under the patronage of the USA slowly and then suddenly escalated into a war whose outcome seems, in retrospect at least, to have been as inevitable as that of the first Indo-China War. The Americans relied heavily on force, blanket bombing, sophisticated modern equipment and superior numbers. They could never accept the fundamental fact that they were engaging with an enemy who was fighting a war of self-determination that had essentially been going on for hundreds of years. Ho Chi Minh was the figurehead of this movement towards independence, the unshakeable conviction of which was rendered in *Apocalypse Now* as the VC's options: 'death or victory'.

Ho Chi Minh embodied – as did Pol Pot, his more fanatical, more extreme counterpart in Cambodia – the ideal of the guerrilla leader of the Vietminh and the Viet Cong, reflected in **Willard**'s narration and emulated by **Kurtz**. From the beginning, Willard admires the VC's discipline in contrast to his own fallibility, 'I am here a week now, waiting for a mission, getting softer. Every minute I stay in this room I get weaker and every minute **Charlie** squats in the bush he gets stronger.' Later, as the **PBR** pulls away from the supply station after the **Playboy Bunnies** scene, Willard comments, 'Charlie didn't get much USO [United Services Overseas]. He was dug in too deep or moving too fast. His idea of great r 'n' r was cold rice and a little rat meat.'

Towards the climax of the film, when Kurtz recalls for Willard his epiphany after the VC had amputated the **polio**-inoculated arms of the Vietnamese boys, he marvels, 'My God, the genius of that. The genius ... the will to do that ... perfect, genuine, complete, crystalline, pure ... Then I realised they were stronger than we ... If I had ten divisions of those men then our troubles here would be over very quickly.' As Ho Chi Minh himself said, 'You can kill ten of my own men for every one I kill of yours. But even at those odds, you will lose and I will win.'

Hollow Men, The

Poem written by **T. S. Eliot** in 1925. As **Willard** recuperates from his imprisonment and the shock of **Chef**'s death, he sits silently in **Kurtz**'s **temple** compound. Kurtz reads:

> We are the hollow men
> We are the stuffed men
> Leaning together
> Headpiece filled with straw. Alas!
> Our dried voices, when
> We whisper together
> Are quiet and meaningless
> As wind in dry grass
> Or rats' feet over broken glass
> In our dry cellar

Shape without form, shade without colour,
Paralysed force, gesture without motion;

Those who have crossed
With direct eyes, to death's other Kingdom.

But then he is drowned out by **the photo-journalist** talking about **dialectics**, before Kurtz throws a book at him to shut him up, and he bows out quoting the poem's end, with the odd amendment:

This is the way the [fuckin'] world ends
[Look at this fuckin' shit we're in, man]
Not with a bang but a whimper.

Immediately after this scene the camera pans across Kurtz's quarters, revealing selected volumes from **Kurtz's library**, and it is here that the referential nature of the film goes a bit berserk. Kurtz misses out the first two lines of the poem for good reason. The epigraph is the manager's boy's announcement to **Marlow** from *Heart of Darkness*:

Mistah Kurtz – he dead.

This creates what we in the field of amateur hermeneutics and semiotics call something of an intertextual conundrum. Kurtz clearly knows the poem well and must have always been rather alarmed at this bald epigraph. On a pedantic note, to extend this idea it must be assumed that an 'outstanding, brilliant' officer, a well-read man, a fan of Eliot and student of his predecessors has also read *Heart of Darkness*. This is absurdly literal.

Like Eliot's *The Waste Land*, this poem expressing the spiritual vacuity of modern life is itself referential, having four key sources: *Heart of Darkness*; Guy Fawkes and the Gunpowder Plot, a theme

introduced in the second epigraph 'A penny for the old guy';
the **assassination** of Julius Caesar as depicted in Shakespeare; and
Dante's *The Divine Comedy*. Eliot himself said that the title was
taken from an amalgam of William Morris's *The Hollow Land* and
The Broken Man by Rudyard Kipling, from whose *If–* the photo-
journalist quotes. It also echoes the description of **Conrad**'s Kurtz
as a 'hollow sham'.

Mention of *The Divine Comedy* – itself drawing on Virgil (see ***The
Golden Bough***, ***Erebus*** and the whole notion of a journey/quest)
– hints at the idea of a mortal confronting hell. The violent deaths
of Guy Fawkes and Julius Caesar clearly anticipate Kurtz's own fate.
The lines

> This is the dead land
> This is the cactus land
> Here the stone images
> Are raised

evoke the 'fuckin' pagan idolatry' referred to by Chef. Perhaps
'Headpiece filled with straw' suggests a hidden link to ***The Wizard
of Oz***. Alas, probably not.

Generally, the poem points to the film's underlying meaning, its
layered structure, the literary, artistic, metaphysical heritage to which
it strives to connect. Also, its absent epigraph has a near-punning
presence, like the title, **the beginning** and **'The End'** pointing out
the film's inevitable conclusion. Finally, its last line must have helped
persuade **Coppola** to rethink his original ending and return to the
more quietly foreboding mood of Conrad's climax, ending not with
a bang but a whimper (an image also borrowed from Kipling).

John Milius recalls that in the place of this poem in his early drafts
was a speech:

about the last hunt of the Mongols, about the circle closing in, and the frenzy of killing. Then the young son of the Khan pulls upon his father's sleeve and says, 'Stop it!' and the Khan declares that the last living thing be allowed to go free. So instead I used that speech at the beginning of *Red Dawn*.

Hopper, Dennis (b. 1936)

Hopper was born in Dodge City, Kansas. As a young actor he became quickly and lastingly obsessed with James Dean, appearing with him in *Rebel Without a Cause* and *Giant*, and he shared and adopted his sense of intensity and rebelliousness. Interestingly (or uninterestingly), there is this Dean link between Hopper, **Sheen** (who impersonated or at least evoked his style in *Badlands*) and **Brando**, to whose position as supreme sexually ambiguous method actor Dean was briefly the pretender. Hopper became notoriously difficult to work with, and his career was in a serious decline when it was temporarily but spectacularly interrupted by *Easy Rider*. This thinly plotted, thickly druggy film of continuingly contested authorship (Hopper, Fonda and the late, great Terry Southern) launched **Jack Nicholson** (a candidate for both **Willard** and **Kurtz**) and made Hopper very rich.

He followed this up with the proto *Apocalypse Now/Heaven's Gate/One From the Heart* self-indulgent disaster/masterpiece *The Last Movie*. What he was really doing – the project that he had commenced in the 1960s, continued with the method dope-smoking scene in *Easy Rider* (according to film lore, over 100 joints were shared by the three actors – is this true/possible/fun?) and his semi-retirement to New Mexico – was ingesting enough **drugs** to facilitate his performance as the Tim Page-like spaced out **photo-journalist** hanging out with Kurtz.

Hopper was originally contracted to play a **Green Beret** sidekick of Kurtz, but when he arrived, a crazed, twittering drug casualty, **Coppola** instantly revised his role and made him the equivalent of the mad harlequin Russian trader from **Conrad**: 'That day, right there, I put the cameras and the **Montagnard** shirt on him, and we shot the scene where he greets them on the **boat**.' Like much in the film, this character and this performance seem at first chaotic and fantastic, but they emerge as not only deliberately funny, but precisely rooted in *Heart of Darkness* and an exercise in methodical madness.

In *Hearts of Darkness: A Filmmaker's Apocalypse* there is a cut from Hopper's effortlessly realised druggy ranting from the film to the articulate, sober, modern, groomed actor saying 'I wasn't in the best shape', which instantly brought the house down at the screening I was at. He actually finishes the sentence 'in terms of my career'. But we shouldn't let that get in the way of the film's best one-liner. By the mid-1970s he had wilfully and chronically abused his body, mind and career, and his eccentric appearance is always jolting: 'For months – for years – his life hadn't been worth a day's purchase – and there he was gallantly, thoughtlessly alive.'

Seeing him in *Hearts of Darkness* reminds you of the effect of watching the film for the first time. There are advantages and disadvantages to watching a film, however great, over and over again. Does the fact that the film's climax improves with each viewing point to its richness or represent a process of inurement to its awkwardness, bizarre acting and **pretentiousness**? Hopper's performance doesn't exactly mellow with repeated viewings, but at least it stands out less starkly.

Coppola, partly to deflect anticipated criticisms about the film's pretentiousness, stated that he was willing to risk pretentiousness. Great, bold art always takes this risk and great films are often partly or nearly bad. It is precisely Dennis Hopper's appearance that marks the beginning of **the end** and the passage of the film which most precariously treads the line between greatness and badness. It also marks the period of Coppola and the film going mad in the **jungle**. However effectively the strange double act of the madman and the fat man emerges in the finished film, it now seems inconceivable that the original plan was to have more – a lot more – of the same, with Hopper and Brando performing endless improvisations. If you consider that what remains is the most controlled and coherent part of this shoot, you feel relieved to have missed out on the four hours of Kurtz's compound material that constituted **Dennis Jakob**'s first cut.

The Hopper that is glimpsed in *Hearts of Darkness* comes over as extremely tricky, with his talent and intelligence mediated by a copious and chronic drug intake. You are confronted with the enduring scene of Coppola in a combination of exasperation and affection explaining to the wilful, childish actor that he has first to learn his lines if he wants to forget them.

Like Brando, Hopper is an iconic figure. His appearance as at least an approximation of himself instantly conveys an out-of-it, out-there quality. His presence emphasises the mood of darkness, drugs and destructiveness of America and the 1960s. He is a **Manson**-like, fried-synapse, psychotic prophet and acolyte. Also, with him as Mr Easy Rider, there is the suggestion that this is some kind of hippie hell.

His performance is funny, mostly deliberately, and is at a different volume and pitch of intensity to any other performance in the film. This is partly because it isn't quite a performance. Like much of his work – exemplified by his now famous phone call to David Lynch to demand the role in *Blue Velvet*, saying 'I am Frank' – it doesn't qualify as acting. Along with his Frank Booth and *Easy Rider*, this is the apotheosis of Dennis Hopper-style acting because it seems to be him being himself. It is a study in volume, gaucheness, pseudo-intellectualism, funny irritating stonedness and a sort of charisma.

In *Neon* magazine, **Laurence Fishburne** remembers a time on location:

Dennis was reading from **the Bible** to me and cutting me a big chunk of hash. He was trying to impress upon me how the angels in the Bible were really spacemen. It was interesting at the time. I was only fifteen.

You want to paraphrase Groucho Marx talking about Chico in *Duck Soup*: 'Dennis Hopper may look mad, act mad, talk mad. But don't let that fool you. He really is mad.'

'The horror! The horror!'

These dying words of **Kurtz**'s are in fact the last eight words of the film as they are repeated when the **boat** travels back down river. They are the last reported words of **Conrad**'s Kurtz, heard by **Marlow** as they head back down river from the Inner Station:

> 'Did he live his life again in every detail of desire, temptation, and surrender during that supreme moment of complete knowledge? He cried in a whisper at some image, at some vision – he cried out twice, a cry that was no more than a breath – "The horror! The horror!"'

Perhaps it is only me finding this numerically ambiguous. When he says 'he cried out twice', does he refer to the two 'The horror!'s or did Kurtz in fact bow out with the more verbose 'The horror! The horror! The horror! The horror!'? In an early cut of the film Brando had improvised a forty-five-minute death speech, which was ultimately, conveniently and probably wisely, contracted to just these four words. The role of these words is more ambiguous in the film than in Conrad. In the film they could conceivably, in part at least, be in reaction to his own violent death, as well as a belated realisation of what he has done. In *Heart of Darkness*, as well as fitting into the book's style of frequent repetitions, the meaning of these last words is strongly suggested by Marlow, who remembers his shock at seeing the impaled **heads** at the Inner Station:

> 'They only showed that Mr Kurtz lacked restraint in the grati-
> fication of his various lusts, that there was something wanting
> in him – some small matter which, when the pressing need

arose, could not be found beneath his magnificent eloquence. Whether he knew of this deficiency himself I can't say. I think the knowledge came to him at last – only at the very last.'

T. S. Eliot initially planned to have 'The horror! The horror!' as the epigraph to *The Waste Land*.

Host, The

A film made by **Coppola**'s fellow UCLA student Jack Hill while he was still at college. Based on ***The Golden Bough***, it features the story of a young man taking refuge in an Aztec **temple** and killing a madman so as to end the drought and save the local people. The director, who went on to make exploitation films in the 1960s and 1970s, recalls:

Francis and I made our student films during the same semester. We all worked on each other's films, but the cameraman on my film also worked on *Apocalypse Now*. I ran into him and I said, 'That looked familiar.' He said, 'Oh yeah, when we were shooting we made jokes about remaking Jack Hill's student film.'

Huey, the

It is Hueys, 'A lot of Hueys', that the crew of the **PBR** see when they first encounter the **Air Cavalry**. The Huey was the main transport and combat **helicopter** used by the Americans in **Vietnam**. It was made by the Bell company and originally named the Iroquois, but was given the name Huey in extension of its technical designation, HU – helicopter utility. Its improved speed, strength and capacity changed the way the Americans waged war. It became a significant combat **weapon**, carrying troops, supplies, boats and cows. It could fire rockets and could, when necessary, remove wounded soldiers from the battlefield and have them in a hospital within fifteen minutes.

I

'(I Can't Get No) Satisfaction'

The Rolling Stones song playing on the radio as **Lance water-skis** behind the **PBR**, announced by the forces DJ as 'a blast from the past'. It was released in the UK in May 1965 and in America in June of the same year. The original plan was to use the Otis Redding cover version.

'I love the smell of napalm in the morning'

The film's most famous line, from one of the most memorable speeches in film history.

After the **napalm** has been dropped to make the point safe enough to **surf, Kilgore** addresses **Lance**:

KILGORE: You smell that? You smell that?
LANCE: Sir?
KILGORE: Napalm, son. Nothing else in the world smells like that.

He then squats down to speak to **Willard**:

I love the smell of napalm in the morning. You know one time we had a hail bomb . . . for twelve hours . . . and when it was all over I walked up. We didn't find one body. Not one stinking **dink** body. But the smell, you know that gasoline smell . . . the whole hill. It smelled like . . . victory. **Some day this war's gonna end.**

It is a short speech in which he confides not to Lance but to Willard, who he thinks might understand, and by the end he is close to tears. This speech bears the **Milius** signature, like a truncated version of his Quint/torpedo/tiger shark World War II speech from *Jaws*, and is possibly inspired by **Michael Herr**'s musings on the distinctive smells of combat in *Dispatches*:

> With all that dust blowing around, the acrid smell of cordite would hang in the air for a long time after firefights, and there was the CS gas that we'd fired at the NVA [North Vietnamese Army] blowing back in over our positions. It was impossible to get a clean breath with all that happening, and there was that other smell too that came up from the shattered heaps of stone wherever an **airstrike** had come in. It held to the lining of your nostrils and worked itself into the weave of your fatigues, and weeks later, miles away, you'd wake up at night and it would be in the room with you.

It also presumably echoes the line from *Heart of Darkness* when **Marlow** has reached the Inner Station:

> 'I felt an intolerable weight oppressing my breast, the smell of the damp earth, the unseen presence of victorious corruption, the darkness of an impenetrable night.'

The first time you hear this speech you assume that he is remembering some brutally effective air strike so successful that all the enemy bodies were vaporised. But of course it is, in fact, an implicit comment on the pointlessness of the American war effort in blanket bombing or inaccurate targeting. It refers to the capture of a nameless, numbered hill that was either unoccupied or abandoned – a part of America's strategy for territorial gains from an enemy which was almost indifferent to such small defeats within the larger context of a struggle for national autonomy. The smell may be pungent but the victory is wholly empty.

The line has attained an iconic status to the extent that any speech referring to the smell of napalm, any line that goes 'I love the smell of . . .' is instantly identifiable as a reference – pastiche or tribute.

If–

The presence of Kipling in the film in the quotation from his poem (as well as much more tangentially in his influence on **The Hollow Men**) is indicative of the film's moral ambiguity and moral balance. With, roughly speaking, **Milius** as Hawk and **Coppola** as, if not quite Dove, then at least a more liberal influence, Kipling represents more of the celebration of the notion of empire than **Conrad** in **Heart of Darkness**. In fact, *The Man Who Would Be King* (Kipling's grim imperial adventure) could be an alternative title for both *Heart of Darkness* and *Apocalypse Now*.

After **the photo-journalist** has boarded the **PBR**, greeting **Willard**, **Lance** and **Chef**, he describes **Kurtz**:

> He's a poet warrior in the classic sense. I mean sometimes he'll, er, when you say hello to him, right, he'll just walk right by you and he won't even notice you and then suddenly he'll grab you and he'll throw you in the corner and he'll say, 'Do you know that if is the middle word in life?'

> If you can keep your head when all about you
> Are losing theirs and blaming it on you,
> If you can trust yourself when all men doubt you

Apart from adding to the literary background of this film (supplying the first hint of the dénouement's densely allusive nature) and supplying a punch-line to a staggeringly uninteresting philosophical/linguistic insight, this is a bit of black humour and a warning to the crew – especially, as it turns out, to Chef – to keep their **heads**.

Ifugao

A **Philippine** tribe drafted in to play **Kurtz**'s **Montagnard** army. As **Eleanor Coppola** writes in *Notes*, there was a rumour on the set that until recently they had been a tribe of head-hunters. They brought to the set an air of authentic tribal ritualism, as they brought with them their authentic rituals. They slaughtered pigs and chickens for purposes of divination as well as eating. From the bile of a chicken, the priest foretold that the work they were doing would be seen around the world and make a lot of money, although there is no evidence that **Francis Coppola** used this evidence to counter negative test screenings. Watching the carnage, **Dennis Hopper** tells Eleanor how he 'kills pigs in New Mexico with a .22 pistol and covers them in shaving cream and shaves their hair off'.

Serendipitously for the film's conclusion, she sees them slaughter a cow; when re-enacted for the cameras this furnishes a counterpoint to the killing of Kurtz.

See **sacrifice**.

'In the Nam of the Father'

In this episode of the cartoon *Duckman* the hero travels to **Vietnam** and has a series of flashbacks lampooning *Forrest Gump*, *The Deer Hunter*, *Good Morning Vietnam*, *Rambo* and *Platoon*. He encounters an inflated version of **Brando**'s **Kurtz**, who tells him:

> You have no right to judge me. You have the right to kill me but not to judge me. Wait, reverse that. Judge me, don't kill me. For no man is an island, though some are roughly the same size. I coulda been somebody. I coulda been a contender.

Senator Corleone. Governor Corleone. We need more butter. General Zog, Krypton will be destroyed. . . . Why am I here, rambling incoherently? The money, the money.

It turns out that the flashbacks are from when he was a National Guardsman projectionist and he got beaten up by female soldiers during a **Vietnam War film** season for showing the porn film *Hard in Darkness*. The latter should not be confused with the genuine porn spin-off movie *Apocalypse Climax* which features the erotic adventures of Captain Willbehard in pursuit of the mysterious Colonel Flirtz.

J

Jakob, Dennis

Credited as creative consultant on the film, Jakob's chief claim is the introduction of **the Fisher King** theme to the conclusion, with **Coppola** actually formulating **the end** during the shoot. Jakob attended the UCLA Film School along with Coppola and Carroll Ballard, and later befriended Jim Morrison, who also studied there. **Walter Murch** recalls Jakob as 'much more somebody who had a personal relationship with Francis than anything else'. He was on the set as 'a kind of cultural advisor, keeping Francis on track with this mythic stuff'. As he had been instrumental in uncovering the key to the film's climax, 'as a just reward Francis said, "Dennis, you edit it."'

So Jakob, having provided the film's inner mythical skeletal structure, went on to assist the film's outer mythology by being very slow at **editing** his allotted section of the film, thereby increasing the film's gestation period. In the creation of the first cut of the film, Murch continues, 'There was the cut up to the compound which was material **Richie [Marks]**, Gerry [Greenberg] and I were working on. But once you got to the **Kurtz** compound, you got into Dennis Jakob's material. His cut alone was four hours long.' Imagine four hours of **Hopper** and **Brando** improvising, extemporising philosophical notions less impressive than the definition of dialectics or the observation that the middle word in life is if.

Since *Apocalypse*, Jakob has, among other things, worked on the script of *Hammett* and helped edit *Koyaanisqatsi*.

Jerry

See Nha Trang, 'Terminate with extreme prejudice' and Ziesmer, Jerry

jungle

When asked why he chose to adapt *Heart of Darkness*, **John Milius** recalled:

> The scene in it where they actually shoot at the continent of Africa. The boat is there firing into the jungle trying to punish the continent of Africa, and that reminded me very much of **Vietnam**. The novel is full of that kind of image of what little effect Victorian culture has on the growth of trees, of how quickly the jungle overcomes everything, how absurd and futile it is for missionaries to go into this dark jungle. This seemed to me to be very like Vietnam.

The jungle in **Conrad** and in *Apocalypse Now* is a consuming power, symbolic of primordial evil and darkness. **Clean** is (unseen in the release version) buried in the jungle, **Chief** has a **water burial**. After the canopy is burnt it is replaced with palm leaves, and when the boat arrives at **Kurtz**'s compound Chief is wearing a palm leaf as a hat.

Johnson, Lance. B

See **Lance**.

Johnson, President Lyndon B.

See **Lance**.

K

Kama, Lieutenant Colonel Pete

One of the military advisers employed on the production. He worked specifically as insignia and infantry operations adviser.

Keitel, Harvey (b. 1941)

Born in Brooklyn. Keitel is one of the busiest leading actors of the last twenty-five years. He was cast as **Willard** but famously lasted only a few days of the shoot. The problems were apparent from the start, as Keitel recalls in *Neon* magazine:

> I was the only person there who knew how to handle the **jungle** – I was the only one who had ever been in the Marines. I don't think we communicated well. We clashed. It was a matter of a young actor who was an ex-marine out of Brooklyn meeting up with a talented director who was out of UCLA and some fraternity.

Coppola also realised rather late that Keitel was incompatible with his vision of the role: 'he found it difficult to play him as a passive onlooker'. Coppola has elaborated on this dramatic recasting, explaining that Willard 'had to be an observer, a watcher. A totally introspective character. In no way could he get in the way of the audience's view of what was happening – of **Vietnam**. That wasn't

going to work with Keitel: his stock in trade is a series of tics – ways
to make people look at him.' This is rather ungracious, almost sadistic,
to obviously miscast an actor, then fire him and mock him for having
star qualities. Coppola was quite aware of the potential significance of
this action: 'Sure, it jeopardises the production, but it can also ruin an
actor's career, to be fired like that.'

Keitel has admitted that 'If I have one god in my life, it's
not going to be Francis Coppola. . . . Had I known then what
I know now, I would have kept my mouth shut longer, and
have them shoot so much they couldn't fire me.' It is almost
certainly a good thing for the film and Keitel's career that he
didn't keep his mouth shut. It is impossible to imagine him as
anything like the impassive Willard as embodied by **Martin Sheen**.
If actors are ever brave, then Harvey Keitel is one of the bravest,
continually nurturing and encouraging new talent – he has probably worked with more first-time directors than any other leading actor.

It is hard to watch his extraordinary performance of guilt, rage and
madness in *Bad Lieutenant* without regarding it as a retroactive audition
for the role of Willard, proof on film that he was prepared to
expose himself to that extent. It is also interesting to compare
Keitel's choices of parts with those of his old friend and colleague
Robert De Niro, who worked so successfully with Coppola on
The Godfather Part II. While De Niro has become increasingly
conservative, Keitel has been ever more extreme, exposing himself (sometimes literally), and alternating between mainstream and
art-house.

Just as François Truffaut used the long gaps while acting in *Close
Encounters of the Third Kind* to write *The Man Who Loved Women*, then
raised finance, shot and released it before *Close Encounters* opened, so
between his firing and *Apocalypse*'s release Keitel made *The Duellists*
(adapted from **Conrad**'s *The Duel*), *Fingers*, *Blue Collar*, *Health* and
Eagle's Wing.

Kilgore (Robert Duvall), Chief (Albert Hall) and Willard (Martin Sheen) around the campfire at the LZ. *'You just knew he wasn't going to get so much as a scratch out there.'*

Robert Duvall, Francis Coppola and Huey.

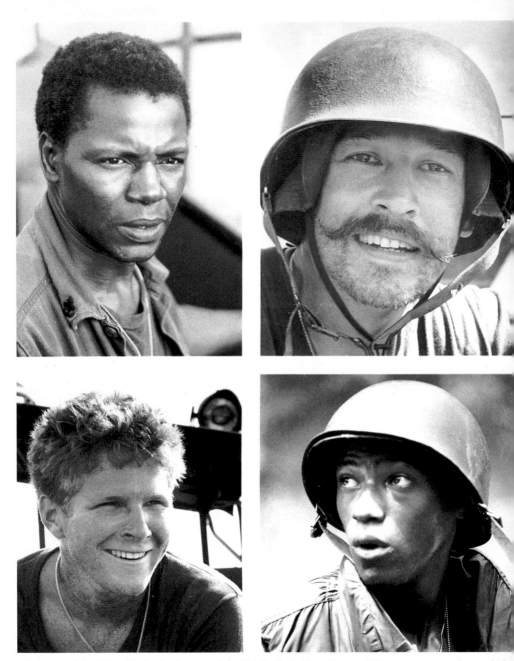

The crew of the PBR. Clockwise from top left: Chief, Chef, Clean, Lance. '*The crew was mostly just kids. Rock 'n' rollers with one foot in the grave.*'

siren.

'he arrival of the Bunnies.

Aurore Clément in the excised French Rubber Plantation sequence.

Do Long Bridge: *The Gates of Hell*.

The final approach to Kurtz's compound.

Our motto: Apocalypse Now.

'I wish I had words.'

The photo-journalist (Dennis Hopper) to Willard: *'Why would a nice guy like you want to kill the genius?'*

Francis and Marlon Brando in one of their frequent conflabs to try and work out Brando's characterisation of Kurtz.

Marlon Brando and Martin Sheen between takes on the set of Kurtz's compound.

Francis Coppola directs the Ifugao tribesmen playing Kurtz's followers.

Marlon Brando as Colonel Walter E. Kurtz.

This is the end.

Kennedy, John F. (1917–63)

The reference to Kennedy in the film is, to say the least, subtle. According to Paul Cullum, in *Film Threat*, who has seen the **five-hour version** of the film:

> At the end of the **surfing** scene, **Lance** steals **Kilgore**'s favourite surfboard, and much levity is had imagining his reaction (at one point, **Willard** – **Martin Sheen**, the perpetual docudrama Kennedy – admonishes them all in an exaggerated Kennedy accent).

Kilgore, Colonel Bill

The commander of the **Air Cavalry** (played by **Robert Duvall**) who is assigned to take **Willard**, the **PBR** and the crew to the mouth of the **Nung river**. While the name clearly suggests the martial, blood-lusting nature of the character (kill + gore, geddit?), it has its source at least partly in *Dispatches*. Michael Herr talks of meeting a **helicopter** gunner who sprayed him with spit when he spoke:

> He was from Kilgore, Texas, and he was on his seventeenth consecutive month in-country.
> 'Why should we do a story about you?'
> 'Cause I'm so fuckin' good,' he said, ''n' that ain't no shit, neither. Got me one hunnert 'n' fifty-se'en **gooks** kilt. 'N' fifty **caribou**.' He grinned and stanched the saliva for a second. 'Them're all certified,' he added.

Kilgore, an apparently outlandish creation, is, like almost everything in the film, grounded in reality. On a surface level, in his rank, uniform and attitude, he is reminiscent of Colonel Custer, the great hero of the US Cavalry, a man made for war. Kilgore's great **'I love napalm in the morning'** speech ends with the film's saddest, perhaps only sad, line, 'Some day this war's gonna end'. This line could have been spoken by the young Custer, who made his reputation thriving in and loving the hateful Civil War and found the subsequent peacetime tedious and frustrating.

The single inspiration for the character is said to be **Colonel John B. Stockton**, himself a great admirer of Custer, although Kilgore is clearly a composite of various people. Certainly Stockton oozes the same bravado and machismo and is utterly devoted to the mythical supremacy of the Air Cavalry. In *Hearts of Darkness: A Filmmaker's Apocalypse* Robert Duvall talks of how the Air Cavalrymen he spoke to would invent little games to spice things up and relieve the boredom, like hooking a bicycle on one of the helicopter's skids in the midst of a raid on a **Viet Cong** village. Stockton, while fiercely protective of the Air Cavalry's reputation, shared this sense of playfulness and revelled in acts of macho improvisation. He was partly responsible for the evolution of the helicopter from an air ambulance into an effective vehicle and **weapon** of war. Serving as an aviation officer in Korea, he customised an H-13 bubble helicopter, an experience which he recalls gleefully, bursting with the fun of the whole enterprise:

> We went out to a hidden valley there, and tied a couple of machine guns on one of the little helicopters. We had a machine gun on each skid, and a little piece of string going from the skid right up to the stick here. We didn't know what was going to happen. There were people who said, 'It's just going to shake the helicopter apart.' I pulled this [the right] string and it started the machine gun going. I pulled this [the left] string and it started this machine gun going, and I learned on my own that if it worked with the little helicopter, it would work with the larger machine.

In his interview with **Eleanor Coppola** in *Notes*:

Bobby [Duvall]talked about basing his character on a West Point officer he knew: a guy whose life only made sense if there was a war. He talked about the details of his costume, the spurs on his boots, his ring, his belt buckle and Stetson hat. He took off his shirt. He was tan and hard. He had his belly sucked in. He ran his hands through his neatly cropped crew-cut hairpiece.

Kilgore is certainly reminiscent of General James F. Hollingsworth, whose exploits were covered in the American press. Nicholas Tomalin wrote a profile of him for *The Sunday Times* in 1966 entitled 'The General Goes Zapping **Charlie** Cong'. Hollingsworth's gung-ho attitude is encapsulated in his statement: 'There's no better way to fight than goin' out to shoot VCs. An' there's nothing I love better than killin' Cong. No sir.'

Although he is shown as a dedicated, consummate soldier, Kilgore is also into games and generally macho fun – he surfs, organises impromptu barbecues, rewards accurate rocket shooting with cases of beer as if at a fun fair, and plays the guitar. The idea of the guitar-playing Air Cavalry officer seems to have been lifted from the newsreel report from the war in which Chief Warrant Officer Wayne Forbes, 'one of America's toughest most daring' and most decorated **Huey** pilots, sings the protest song he has written. Unlike most protest songs of the period, this one calls for more violence and ruthlessness from the Americans in **Vietnam**.

Also, Coppola's insight from his experience writing the screenplay for *Patton*, about the brilliant, eccentric American General of World War II, seeped into the characterisation of Kilgore and, to a lesser extent, Willard and **Kurtz**. Like the other characters in the film, Kilgore is partly an invention, partly a composite, partly representative of a type – he is really a typically goof-ball Air Cavalry officer cultivating his own reputation for eccentric bravado and adopting a pragmatic xenophobia. General Patton's son, unsurprisingly named George S. Patton Jr, served as an Air Cavalry colonel in the

Vietnam War. He once said, 'Boys, I don't have anything against the Vietnamese personally, but I sure do like to see those arms and legs fly.'

Kilgore represents the tradition of great, mad American soldiers. He is popular with his men ('He loved his boys and they felt safe with him'), although he encourages them to surf during a battle. He is the film's most charismatic character and its most **racist**. He is the only man to use every available nickname and abusive term for the VC – Charlie, **dink**, gook, **slope** and one of his own, 'fucking savages' – and at the same time he appreciates and applauds an enemy soldier brave enough to fight with his guts hanging out.

As he struts around the beach bare chested and apparently oblivious to the shells dropping all around him, you know he won't get hurt. This near-comic (it is reminiscent of the banquet at the end of *Carry On Up the Khyber*) but absolute invulnerability has already been pointed out by Willard, observing him relaxing at the beach barbecue: 'He was one of those guys who have that weird light around him. You just knew that he wasn't going to get so much as a scratch here.' Being lucky, as Napoleon pointed out, is one of a general's (or colonel's) most important attributes, and it was in this near-mystical form that **Michael Herr** became acutely aware of it in Vietnam. He encounters the phenomenon in several guises. First there is the soldier Orrin, who is determined to return home to kill his unfaithful wife:

> After that, he was the crazy fucking grunt who was going to get through the war so he could go home and kill his old lady. It made him someone special in the company. It made a lot of guys think that he was lucky now, that nothing could happen to him, and they stayed as close to him as they could. I even felt some of it, enough to be glad that we would be in the same bunker that night. It made sense. I believed it too, and I would have been really surprised if I had heard later that anything had happened to him.

Then there is the young Marine wandering around the damaged helicopter without a safety line:

> At 1,500 feet he stood there in the gale-sucking door (Did he ever think about stepping off? How often?), his hands resting naturally on his hips, as though he were just standing on a street corner somewhere, waiting. He knew he was good, an artist, he knew we were digging it, but it wasn't for us at all; it was his, private; he was a man who was never going to fall out of any damn helicopter.

Then there is a helicopter journey during which Herr sits next to a young Marine reading **the Bible**. Herr offers him a cigarette. The Marine nervously refuses, but returns the gesture of friendship by pointing to a passage from the Bible, Psalms 91:5:

Thou shalt not be afraid for the **terror** by night; nor for the **arrow** that flieth by day.
Nor for the pestilence that walketh in darkness; nor for the destruction that wasteth at noonday.
A thousand shall fall at thy side, and ten thousand at thy right hand; but it shall not come nigh thee.

The Bible is an underlying presence in the film. Finally, looking back on his time in Vietnam, Herr recalls:

> I was no more superstitious than anyone else in Vietnam, I was very superstitious, and there were always a few who seemed so irrefutably charmed that nothing could make me picture them lying dead there.

This quality of inviolability makes Kilgore as mythical a figure as Kurtz. Kilgore embodies the values of eccentricity, playfulness, ruthlessness and madness of the real American war effort in Vietnam. Colonel Stockton is certainly not ashamed to be introduced as the inspiration for Kilgore. As exaggerated and fictional as he seems, as insanely skewed in his priorities, and as openly racist in his language, Kilgore's charisma and power of personality are such that he briefly takes over the film. He is Custer, Stockton, Polyphemus the Cyclops and also, in his equal infatuation with warfare and surfing, he is John Milius.

See **Odyssey, The**.

Kurtz

Kurtz, the star ivory trader gone native and mad in **Heart of Darkness**, becomes Colonel Walter E. Kurtz, the star soldier gone native and mad in *Apocalypse Now*. The climatic arrival, **the end** of the quest, is, inevitably, partly anti-climax, especially on a journey in both book and film that explicitly promises to end with the encounter with a great man. Kurtz, in book and film, is a man who derives his power from the brilliance of his words as much as his deeds, so the writer in both cases is presented with the dilemma of whether to attempt to present a kind of religious text or the suggestion of this universal genius. **Conrad** plumps directly for the latter. It says something about the madness, the ludicrous ambition of the *Apocalypse Now* project that for a long time its makers attempted to pull off the former.

In *Heart of Darkness* **Marlow** is first informed of Kurtz by **the Company**'s chief accountant, who says of him simply 'He is a very remarkable person.' Marlow learns that he is in charge of a very important trading post, the Inner Station: 'Oh, he will go far, very far,' he began again. 'He will be somebody in the Administration before long. They, above – the Council in Europe, you know – mean him to be.' As he continues, Marlow hears rumours that Kurtz is ill. The manager of the Central Station assures him that 'Kurtz was the best agent he had, an exceptional man, of the greatest importance to the Company'. Kurtz slowly emerges as a Renaissance man, a painter, 'He is a prodigy . . . an emissary of pity, and science, and progress, and devil knows what else. [He embodies] intelligence, wide sympathies, a singleness of purpose. [He is] a special being.' But still Marlow doesn't have a picture of Kurtz, 'no more than if I had been told an angel or a fiend was in there'. Gradually, an image of Kurtz emerges through the rumours and anecdotes, until suddenly, after the death of the helmsman, Marlow supposes that Kurtz is dead too:

> 'I couldn't have been more disgusted if I had travelled all this way for the sole purpose of talking with Mr Kurtz. Talking with . . . I fling one shoe overboard, and became aware that that was exactly what I had been looking forward to – a talk with Kurtz. I made the strange discovery that I had never imagined him as doing, you know, but as discoursing. I didn't say to myself, 'Now I will never see him,' or 'Now I will never shake him by the hand,' but, 'Now I will never hear him.' The man presented himself as a voice. Not of course that I did not connect him with some sort of action. Hadn't I been told in all the tones of jealousy and admiration that he had collected, bartered, swindled, or stolen more ivory than all the other agents together? That was not the point. The point was in his being a gifted creature, and that of all his gifts the one that stood out pre-eminently, that carried with it a sense of real presence, was his ability to talk, his words – the gift of expression, the bewildering, the illuminating, the most exalted and the most contemptible, the pulsating stream of light, or the deceitful flow from the heart of an impenetrable darkness.'

Before in his account he has reached the Inner Station he introduces the listeners to Kurtz's head:

> 'And the lofty frontal bone of Mr Kurtz! They say the hair goes on

growing sometimes, but this – ah – specimen was impressively bald. The wilderness had patted him on the head, and, behold, it was like a ball – an ivory ball.'

Kurtz talked of '"My ivory, my intended, my station, my river, my –" everything belonged to him . . . He had taken a high seat among the devils of the land – I mean literally.' Marlow talks of how Kurtz was exposed to temptations in the **jungle**, temptations that most people could not understand: 'His mother was half-English, his father half-French. All Europe contributed to the making of Kurtz.'

Marlow reads the report that he was commissioned to write for the International Society for the Suppression of Savage Customs and, although he again talks of his words as 'eloquent, vibrating with eloquence', he briefly quotes the extract referring to whites as 'supernatural beings'. The postscript is concise: 'Exterminate all the brutes!'

Much of what we learn in the fragmented, impressionistic portrait of Kurtz is from the staccato account of the Russian trader: 'We talked of everything. . . . Everything! Everything! Everything! . . . Of love, too . . . He made me see things . . . he raided the country. . . . They [the tribe] adored him. . . . What can you expect? . . . he came to them like thunder.' Marlow says, 'I hadn't heard any of these splendid monologues on, what was it? on love, justice, conduct of life – or what not.'

When he and we finally encounter Kurtz borne on a stretcher, we get a reasonably vivid physical description of the man:

'I saw the thin arm extended commandingly, the lower jaw moving, the eyes of that apparition shining darkly far in its bony head that nodded with grotesque jerks. Kurtz – Kurtz – that means short in German – don't it? Well, the name was as true as everything else in his life – and death. He looked at least seven feet long. His covering had fallen off, and his body emerged from it pitiful and appalling as from a winding-sheet. I could see the cage of his ribs all astir, the bones of his arms waving. It was as though an animated image of death carved out of old ivory had been shaking its hand with menaces at a motionless crowd of men made of dark and glittering bronze. I saw him open his mouth wide – it gave him a weirdly voracious aspect, as though he had wanted to swallow all the air, all the earth, all the men before him. A deep voice reached me faintly.'

Marlow has caught his first sight of the object of his journey, quest and obsession at a distance through binoculars, so he sees him and sees him speak before the words reach his hearing. **Willard** also first views the compound through binoculars, and this effect of separate but simultaneous introduction to Kurtz's face and voice is also replicated in *Apocalypse Now* when, before receiving his mission, he is shown an old photo of Kurtz, and played a tape of two communications monitored out of Cambodia on 9 October and 30 December 1968 and verified as being of his voice. The first goes thus:

I watched a snail crawl along the edge of a straight razor. That's my dream, it's my nightmare . . . crawling along the edge of a straight razor . . . and surviving.

This is just a little bit mad (taken, as is the second communication, from **Brando**'s lengthy improvisations, much of which made it into **Dennis Jakob**'s first cut but survive in the final film only in fragments), and already hints at the interlinked destinies of Kurtz and Willard, Kurtz's death wish and **the Fisher King** theme. The second communication, Kurtz's version of 'Happy New Year', seals it:

But we must kill them, we must incinerate them, pig after pig, cow after cow, village after village, army after army. And they call me an **assassin**. What do you call it when the assassins accuse the assassin? They lie. They lie and we have to be merciful with those who lie. Those nabobs. I hate them. I do hate them.

The General supplies some background:

> Walter Kurtz was one of the most outstanding officers this country has ever produced. He was brilliant, he was outstanding in every way. And he was a good man too, a humanitarian man. A man of wit and humour. He joined the Special Forces and after that his ideas, his methods, became unsound. Unsound.

He and the Colonel go on to explain how Kurtz has crossed over into Cambodia with his **Montagnard** army, who treat him like a god. He is about to be arrested for the murder of four South Vietnamese agents whom he suspected as double agents. There is, as he memorably says, a battle in every man between good and evil, and good does not always triumph. Every man has a breaking point; Kurtz has reached his and has obviously gone insane.

Willard, already hooked, pauses significantly before feeling obliged to agree: 'Yes, sir. Very much so, sir. Obviously insane.' Willard accepts this non-existent mission, to **terminate with extreme prejudice** Kurtz's command: 'What the hell else was I going to do?'

He has heard Kurtz's name even before the mission, but it is the voice that 'put the hooks' in him. Although, as in *Heart of Darkness*, Kurtz's is only a brief, mysterious physical presence towards the climax, he dominates the story, and details of his character and history unfold during the journey up river. The device for this gradual revelation in the film is that of Willard leafing through his mission dossier between adventures on the voyage. These insert sequences were filmed in the Napa Valley in California after the location shooting in **the Philippines**. On the **PBR** we catch a glimpse of his career file:

46   Graduates West Point; second in Class; third generation appointee. Completes Basic Training, Advanced Infantry Training, Fort Gordon, Georgia.

47–48   Assigned, West Berlin, U.S. Sector Command, G–I (Plane) Promoted 1st Lt.

49–50   Masters Degree, Harvard University, History (Thesis: The Philippines Insurrection: American Foreign Policy in South-east Asia, 1898–1905).

50–51   Assigned General Staff, U.S. Command, Seoul, Korea: Combat Zones, Division Evaluation Team.
Requests transfer to Intelligence: returned U.S. for special training, Ft. Holabird and Washington.
(Marries, Janet Anderson, 14 June 1951.)
Returns to active duty, G–2, Seoul: Debriefs and evaluates information from American agents returning from Northern missions.
Promoted Captain.

As he reads, Willard comments:

Third generation West Point. Top of his class. Korea. Airborne. About a thousand decorations etc. etc. I'd heard his voice on the tape and it really put the hook in me. [Is this a play on the role of Kurtz as Fisher King?] But I couldn't connect up that voice with this man. Like they said, he had an impressive career. Maybe too impressive. I mean perfect. He was being groomed

for one of the big slots in the Corporation – General, Chief of
Staff, anything.

In 1964, he returned from a tour with Advisory Command,
Vietnam and things started to slip. His report [entitled 'Status of
United States Involvement in the Republic of South Vietnam']
to the Joint Chiefs of Staff and **Lyndon Johnson** was restricted.
It seems they didn't dig what he had to tell 'em.

He made three requests for transfer to Airborne. We briefly see these
three requests, the third one authorised, having been accompanied by
a letter to his superior officer and friend:

> You have known me for eighteen years. Long enough to know
> that I will not and cannot change my mind. This is my third
> attempt, and three's the magic number.
>   Humor me, Willie,
>
> Walt

Willard reads: '1966 Joined Special Forces. Returns Vietnam.' He
was 38-years old. As Willard points out, the next-oldest person on
the training course was half his age – 'I did it when I was nineteen.
It damn near finished me. Tough mother-fucker.' In October 1967
he improvised Operation **Archangel**, a triumph picked up on by the
media, which led to him being made a full colonel. Willard says:

> Late Summer/Autumn 1968 – Kurtz's patrols coming under
> frequent attacks. The camp started falling apart. November,
> Kurtz ordered the assassination of three Vietnamese men and one
> **woman**. Two of them were colonels in the South Vietnamese
> Army. Enemy activity in his old sector dropped off to nothing.
> Guess he must have hit the right four people.

He reports how the army tried to reel Kurtz back in, but he kept on playing by his own rules and winning, and he began making hit-and-run raids into Cambodia. Willard reads out the letter Kurtz sent to his son:

Dear Son,

I am afraid that both you and your mother will have been worried at not hearing from me during the past weeks, but my situation here has become a difficult one. I have been officially accused of murder by the Army.

The alleged victims were four Vietnamese agents. We spent months uncovering them and accumulating evidence. When absolute proof was completed, we acted. We acted like soldiers. The charges are unjustified. They are, in fact, and in the circumstances of this conflict, quite completely insane.

In a war there are many moments for compassion and tender action. There are many moments for ruthless action, what is often called ruthless, what may in many circumstances be only clarity, seeing clearly what there is to be done and doing it directly, quickly, aware, looking at it.

I will trust you to tell your mother what you choose about this letter. As for the charges against me, I am unconcerned. I am beyond their timid, lying morality and so I am beyond caring.

You have all my faith,

Your Loving
Father

Here again the film returns to the theme of **lies**. Willard is establishing some mystical, primal link with Kurtz. When he has shocked the PBR crew by finishing off the wounded woman on the **sampan** he knows that he has learnt something about Kurtz that wasn't in his dossier. After the death of **Clean** they draw closer and see the river banks strewn with corpses:

He was close. He was real close. I couldn't see him yet, but I
could feel him, as if the boat were being sucked upriver and the
water was flowing back into the jungle.

When he first enters the **temple** he is struck by the smell – malaria,
the disease that kills Conrad's Kurtz. It is in appearance that the two
Kurtzes most starkly differ from each other. Both are bald and dying,
but, while Conrad's Kurtz is 'long, pale indistinct, like a vapour
exhaled by the earth', Brando's Kurtz is far from wasting away. His
exhalation would have to be the result of a very deep breath. Whatever
justifications and compensations have been made (no full body shots
and wonderfully appropriate lighting, with Kurtz drifting in and out
of darkness, and a tall stand-in for long shots and silhouettes), it just
doesn't quite make sense that this ruthlessly efficient, highly trained
soldier should be so fat. Perhaps they could have named him Klein
('Klein – that means skinny in German, don't it?'; Klein was Conrad's
original name for Kurtz). There is an inevitable sense of anti-climax
at the conclusion of any quest, and it was to counter this that the film
needed a star of Brando's stature at the end of the river, but not that
kind of stature.

Conrad's Kurtz remains mysterious in speech. He says very
little, although he is known for having 'A voice! A voice!' The
reader is told of his speech and writings without knowing what
he actually says and writes, beyond brief extracts. As when they
depart from the Inner Station, Marlow says simply, 'Kurtz dis-
coursed.' *Apocalypse Now*'s Kurtz has to talk more and so becomes
more fixed, more concrete, more revealed. Still, he doesn't say
much. He asks Willard about where he grew up and talks about
travelling through a **gardenia** plantation on the **Ohio river** as a
child. He asks Willard: 'Have you ever considered real freedom?'
There is a brief suggestion that what he is doing represents total
freedom – the freedom to exercise his own will, realise his ideas
and desires.

There is then the questioning of his **method**, taken almost straight from *Heart of Darkness*, and the revelation of Willard as assassin/soldier/delivery boy. It is hard to see the scene of Kurtz dropping **Chef**'s **head** in Willard's lap as anything but pure plagiarism. Fortunately it was plagiarised from *The Godfather*, the supreme act of power and intimidation in the form of the trophy head presented to the victim, who reacts with a scream of primal terror. This segues into Kurtz's final scene. After his recitation of *The Hollow Men*, Kurtz explains that 'It is impossible to describe what is necessary to those who don't know what horror means. . . . Horror has a face. . . . Horror and moral **terror** are your friends.'

He then relates his own epiphany when he witnessed the genius, the will of the **Viet Cong**, when they hacked off the inoculated arms of the children in the village, apparently a genuine incident witnessed by **John Milius**'s friend and one of the film's military advisers, **Fred Rexer**. He concludes: 'I worry that my son might not understand what I've tried to be', and entrusts Willard as the **caretaker** of his memory.

Kurtz is recognisably based upon Conrad's creation, in exactly the same way that the film in general has clear roots in the novel. He is considerably fleshed out, and he has been updated and made more specific to his time, in a similar way to what Orson Welles had planned for his proposed adaptation. But where Welles drew explicit parallels between Kurtz and Hitler, in the post-Vietnam era there is no clear division between good and evil, friend and enemy. Kurtz has been seduced by, and now takes his orders from, the primal force of the jungle. He is a good, humanitarian man whose absolute and obvious insanity manifests itself in the form of pure warfare. He has seen through the hypocrisy and utter ineffectuality of the American war effort, and has simply assessed the ultimate aims of his own side and gone mad while pursuing these ends and adopting the methods, philosophy and pure will of the Viet Cong.

Apocalypse Now is an absurdly ambitious film wanting to tackle the same issues as *Heart of Darkness* and more. It addresses the morality of war, imperialism, the struggle between good and evil, weaves in sex, **drugs**, **rock 'n' roll**, references to dozens of films, books, poems and myths. To what degree it succeeds and fails is of course down to individual taste, but, undeniably, if nothing else it offers a great ride. The conclusion is almost wilfully inchoate, wanting to present and draw upon so many things simultaneously. One can't be wholly persuaded by Kurtz, although on some viewings one gets close, and this may well be largely down to the *Wizard of Oz* problem. You can't forget that it is an overweight Marlon Brando as a lean fighter, twittering on in his mercifully abbreviated attempts to lose himself in a characterisation of pure evil.

The background to the part has something, though. It has exaggerated mystery and the repeated suggestion that this mystery may be a puzzle with a solution. Certainly in his **polio**/will speech there is a substance, an impetus to the role which completes a triumvirate of characters begun by Willard and **Kilgore**, who together offer an undeniably more profound and interesting vision of America's involvement in Vietnam than those in, say, *The Deer Hunter*, *Coming Home* and *Platoon*, and arguably a more truthful one.

Kurtz's library

Kurtz's library, or what we see of it – **Goethe**, **the Bible**, *From Ritual to Romance*, *The Golden Bough* and *The Collected Poems of T. S. Eliot* – is mainly there for symbolic reasons, to suggest literary and mythical connections. But how realistic is it that these books should be available there? James Fenton, the poet and journalist, who covered the fall of **Saigon**, said this was quite feasible, that these were precisely the kinds of books that people carried around and exchanged. In *Dispatches*, **Michael Herr** records the life of Saigon cafés frequented by 'Vietnamese "students" . . . reading Pléiade editions of Proust, Malraux, Camus'.

L

Lance

Gunner's Mate 3rd Class Lance B. Johnson. 'He was a famous surfer from the beaches south of LA. To look at him you wouldn't believe he'd ever fired a **weapon**.' The lance is one of the key symbols (phallic, of course) explored in **Jessie L. Weston**'s *From Ritual to Romance*, one of the few books shown to be in **Kurtz's library**. Also, as is made explicit when **Chef** hands him his letter delivered at the **Do Long bridge** addressed to 'L. B. Johnson', in name only he evokes the president responsible for America's escalating involvement in **Vietnam** from late 1963 onwards, Lyndon Baines Johnson. In fact, according to **John Milius**, both these links began as happy coincidences. As he says, 'There was a real famous surfer, a real good friend of mine called Lance Carson. As a matter of fact the character in *Big Wednesday* is called Matt Johnson, and he is also a version of Lance Carson.'

He is the film's conscience and symbol of innocence. He brings, along with **Clean**, the trappings of American youth lifestyle to Vietnam. He smokes **dope**, drops **acid**, surfs, **water-skis to rock 'n' roll**, adopts a **puppy** (this seems at first a little silly and unsubtle – the puppy is not a famously understated symbol of innocence – but, like so much here, this is based on documentary evidence, newsreel footage of grunts taking Labrador puppies into combat under their jackets), thinks he's in **Disneyland**, and gradually, along with the other crew members and the boat, is consumed and corrupted by the primal force of the **jungle**. He is the first to assume **camouflage** so they can't see him (he is right, they are everywhere – he knows this intuitively even before **Willard**); he howls at the invisible enemy. Lance has a mystical bond with the water, and it is he who performs the ritualistic **water burial** of **Chief** Phillips.

At the compound he is almost at once absorbed into **Kurtz**'s band. He performs some kind of idiosyncratic Tai Chi in the background while Kurtz talks to Willard, and he even helps ready the **carabao** for **sacrifice**. After Kurtz's assassination Lance briefly becomes Nathalie Wood in a re-enactment of the end of *The Searchers*. There Ethan Edwards (John Wayne), having spent ten years trying to rescue his niece, Debbie (Wood), is resolved to kill her as she has been corrupted by the savages, animals, and is 'living with a Comanche buck' (Scar). On seeing her, he suddenly changes his mind and sweeps her up in his arms and tells her: 'Debbie, we're going home.' Likewise in *Apocalypse Now*, with the death of Kurtz (Scar, the Wicked Witch) the spell is broken and Willard retrieves the zombified Lance; together they head off home and into the heart of an immense darkness. *The Searchers* is also the key model for the John Milius production *Uncommon Valor*, in which a team of Vietnam vets (and Patrick Swayze) led by the near-**Kilgore Gene Hackman**, rescue American prisoners of war still in a Vietnamese camp years after the end of the war.

Lance, surprisingly for a younger surfer, but like Kilgore, prefers a heavier board – you can't ride the nose with a lighter one – and has the best cut-back there is.

last words

In the completed film the last words spoken are the repeated dying words of **Kurtz** (the same last words as **Conrad**'s Kurtz), **'The horror! The horror!'** The original plan was for a much, much longer final speech. **Brando** did two forty-five-minute improvisations of this speech. The second take was used to supply snippets included in the final version, such as the extracts played to **Willard** in the lunch/mission meeting in **Nha Trang**. The first goes like this:

I . . . I . . . I had . . . I had immense plans. I was on the threshold of great things. And what you've hacked here to the ground like a tree is not **the end** of it. No, you've also shaken the seeds from that tree. And I will take root in you. I will sprout. I will be nourished by your violence. Nothing. Nothing. To look into the abyss without drawing away is everything. The highest . . . The highest of honours. To approach the horizon of endurable anguish and to pass it, you must have eyes without eyelids, for if you blink once you will incinerate.

We will win this war. We are winning it. And you will . . . you will help to win it. And just beneath the surface is your strength. Just below your skin are your vital forms, your vital forces running like eternal springs. Wild. Restless. They will guide you, and give you counsel.

And when they call you a murderer, and when they judge you, then turn on them, hang them, all of them, by their lying jaws on meathooks till they soil themselves and ask forgiveness. The bloodlust. The bloodlust – you don't think of it. You don't think of the bloodlust; you experience it. Masses . . . people – any people – they will go anywhere, do anything, as long as the ring of faith . . . the ring of faith is in their noses. Yes. Put the rings in their nose. Call it God. And Country. And Mother. Then you run a slim cord through the rings of all of them – ten million, a hundred million or more – and herd them wherever you will.

The human animal has no limits. He will generate a force to overcome the gravitational pull of society and fling himself into outer space to find a new orbit around Jupiter or the Sun, determined by far greater forces. And the instinct to submission

is stronger than the will to power . . . Eichmann . . . Eichmann
. . . Six million Jews jumped into their graves . . . Düsseldorf
. . . Bremen . . . Wounded Knee . . . Coventry . . . Nagasaki . . .
Ten-year-old boys carrying . . . carrying grenades in baskets of
fruit. And pregnant women, nursing women, carrying explosives
in their vaginas . . . inside their vaginas, crossing beyond our
checkpoints.

Extremism in the defence of liberty is no vice . . . No . . .
No vice . . . No vice . . .

This war will never be won by priests of misery, the Rand
Corporation and not in the Situation Rooms in Washington.
The people here, those yellow and white who lie in the muck
and who can't stand the rain and no food, the stink and the
rot of dying . . . People who get sick and wake up numb and
still have the will to fight. They're the ones who will stand it.
And the ones . . . and the ones who will win . . . None other
. . . None other . . . They just need the will, the guns and the
grace of God. The enemy, well-trained, experience no fear. VC
[**Viet Cong**] gun . . . NVA . . . [North Vietnamese Army] . . .
no fear in their gun . . . Not in their gun. Their minds have fear
of their minds. You hack them to pieces and they say nothing.
They only inspire respect. God help you if you . . . God help
you. The strong . . . the strongest leaders don't want to lose this
war to little yellow men in black pyjamas, so they lie. Presidents,
all of them, all the Presidents, want to retain power, so they lie.
Congressmen, our . . . **lies**. Lies. Magazines . . . lies.

This is not a war of people and freedom and rights and
self-determination. Lies. Only oil, power, manganese, cobalt,
geopolitics, staying in office . . . must have these . . . we must
have these . . . lies. Remain strong. Remain free. Regret . . .
regret . . . never saw a flower being pushed into the end of
AK-47 muzzle. Children put their flowers where I can see
them. I'd like to see their faces if they'd put the flowers

in VC guns. The top of their heads would come off . . . [incomprehensible] . . . Lies . . . Lies.

They are right. They are right. We should not intervene. No intervention here. Civil war. Their war. No intervention. They are right. Not intervene, but to invade, inundate all of Southeast Asia with fire enough to eliminate . . . eliminate our intentions here for two centuries. They don't want my mission to succeed because they would be wrong, and they would rather be dead . . . dead than wrong.

No. Stay with the primitive here. Stay with these people. Stay with them. They're small feathers in this hurricane of change, this whirlwind. But they know, they understand, they're made of the earth. They live without fear. They do not hide in masks of guilt. Platinum. Platinum. There are some things, there are some things of which I cannot, I dare not speak.

To raise a stench, a stench so strong as to break the stride of . . . of a pack of jackals. To be as familiar with death as maggots are with manure. The world needs us now, and we will stay here until mushrooms grow out of our faces. These men, these tired ticks that crawl across . . . across the anvil of history. A time for giants, and they send us pygmies armed with chalk, computers, tennis rackets, Santa Monica hotlines to human misery. The eager students of suffering and violence. The sick and twisted hippies, long-haired hypocrites, rotting with decay. In every powerful civilisation for the past 35 centuries, violence stills those inner ancient passions, that primordial slime that lies in the bottom of our minds waiting aeons and aeons to be . . . only to be stirred and − what? And the silkworms . . . the silkworms writing those fawning reports of victories while we die out here like blind martins. The experts, the air conditioned priests, who only look for the break point in human misery. McNamara . . . Bunker . . . Rostow . . . Bunker . . . Bundy . . . Bunker . . . Bunker . . . Johnson.

lies

You know I hate, detest, and can't bear a lie, not simply because I am
straighter than the rest of us, but simply because it appals me.

Marlow in *Heart of Darkness*

The lie is a central theme in the film. When **Willard** first hears
Kurtz's voice one of the things that puts the hook in him is his
anger at the hypocrisy in the war: 'They lie. . . . They lie and we
have to be merciful with those who lie.' This has two meanings,
referring to the double agents, but mainly to the lies of the military
establishment in **Vietnam**. They are nabobs, opportunists gaining
wealth from colonial occupation. Willard empathises with Kurtz; he
is equally contemptuous of the military leaders, 'Four star clowns who
were going to end up giving the whole circus away'. His narration
continually points out different forms of hypocrisy. As soon as he
has accepted his mission he wonders at the point of it, saying that
charging someone with murder in Vietnam was like 'handing out
speeding tickets at the Indy 500'. Later, as the **PBR** starts its journey
up river, leaving **Kilgore** and the **Air Cavalry** at the temporarily
captured point, Willard says, 'If that's the way Kilgore fought the war,
I was beginning to wonder what they had against Kurtz.' You need
wings to stay above the **bullshit**. Lies are also a feature of **Brando**'s
improvised death speech.

A film that carefully avoids direct political content in its final
version is no less graphic in its presentation, through the words and
actions of (to varying degrees) madmen, the untenability, incoherence
and insanity of America's policy and involvement in the **Vietnam
War**. *Apocalypse Now*'s Kurtz pursues the war in the same ruthlessly
efficient way that **Conrad**'s Kurtz gathers ivory. He is driven mad
by the forces in the **jungle** connecting with his own primal desires,
but also by the nature of the war and the army's refusal to wage it
honestly. He is ultimately condemned, not for his savagery – largely

an extension of and indistinguishable from other military activity – but for his refusal to be reeled in, to conform to what he sees as the army's lies. He lacks restraint and sound **methods**.

Coppola himself, typically identifying with his characters, also became obsessed with the notion of the lie during the shoot. He initially regarded **the end** of the film which made it to the final release version as not merely a compromise but a lie. Coppola is consciously or otherwise losing himself so much in the project that he sounds uncannily, ludicrously like Brando as Kurtz. Interviewed on location, Coppola was asked if he was making an anti-war film. He replied, 'It's not an anti-war movie. It's an anti-lie movie.'

lighting

See **Storaro, Vittorio**.

Lombardi, Joseph

Special effects co-ordinator born in Passaic, New Jersey. He has worked extensively in TV (*I Love Lucy* and *I Spy*, among others) and film (*The Valachi Papers* and *Obsession*, as well as the first two *Godfather* films.) At the time he considered the effects in *Apocalypse Now* to have been 'the biggest explosive show ever devised for film', although of course his biggest explosion didn't quite make it to the official version of the completed film. In the **Do Long bridge** sequence alone Lombardi and his special effects crew used more than 500 smoke bombs, 100 phosphorous sticks, 1,200 gallons of gas, 50 water explosions of 35 sticks of dynamite each, 2,000 rockets, flares, tracers and 5,000 feet of detonating cord. For the **napalm** raid they used 2,000 gallons of petrol. Thousands of smoke cans costing $25 each were used in the production, particularly around the **temple** complex.

As **Eleanor Coppola** writes in *Notes*: 'Joe said there won't be another show with effects this big for a long time. There are a couple of his crew in their mid-sixties. He let them set off the biggest phases of the explosions on the last night at **Kurtz**'s temple. He said they'd never get an opportunity like that again in their lifetimes. One of his men, Jerry [Endler], worked on *Cleopatra* and *The Sand Pebbles* and some of the biggest productions, but "nothing came close to this show in terms of effects".'

Lombardi summed up thus: 'I served one hitch in the Pacific in '42, and another one there with Francis. It was the chance of a lifetime.'

Love Song of J. Alfred Prufrock, The

When **the photo-journalist** greets the **PBR** with his rapid-fire delivery he compares himself to **Kurtz**:

I'm a little man, I'm a little man, he's a great man, er, er,
I should have been a pair of ragged claws (er)
Scuttling across the floors of silent seas.

These last two lines are from **T. S. Eliot**'s *The Love Song of J. Alfred Prufrock* and themselves refer to Hamlet's feigned madness, which, as well as reinforcing his obeisance to Kurtz, perhaps suggests that the photographer is affecting his extreme eccentricity, playing the fool to survive.

Lucas, Colonel G.

See **Colonel, the**.

Lucas, George (b. 1944)

Writer, producer and director born in Modesto, California (the setting for *American Graffiti*). At University of Southern California Film School he made a short version of *THX 1138*, which he would expand and remake as his feature debut. His uneasy, love/hate relationship with **Coppola** began in the summer of 1967, when he won a student competition, the prize for which was to attend the shooting of any Warner Bros film. The only film being shot on the Burbank lot was *Finian's Rainbow*. The two men became friends almost at once, with Lucas cast as the protégé to the not much older but successful and established Coppola. Coppola secured a production deal for the dark (well, bright but cheerless) *THX 1138* as part of a package of projects for Warner Bros.

This dystopian sci-fi vision was unsurprisingly a commercial flop. Lucas's second film, *American Graffiti*, produced by Coppola and featuring **Harrison Ford** as the new racer in town, became one of the most financially successful films up to that time. But during this project the friendship between Lucas and Coppola was already becoming strained, and Lucas never forgave Coppola for what he saw as unfair allotment of the film's profits.

Apocalypse Now began as a joint project initiated by Lucas and **John Milius** at USC. As **Walter Murch** recalls, 'It was a project that George and John Milius had cooked up. I think John was initially responsible for it. They were preparing it in the very early days of American **Zoetrope**. The plan was that George would finish *THX 1138* and would go on to *Apocalypse Now*. At that time the war was still on.'

Already at this early stage the project had Lucas supplying a liberal counter-balance to Milius's more right-wing inclinations. As Dale Pollock writes in *Skywalking: The Life and Films of George Lucas*, Milius saw the film as being 'about shitkicking the enemy whether it was justified or not. Lucas saw the movie as an updated *Dr Strangelove*, a case of trying to kill an ant with a sledgehammer, only to discover that the ant is winning.'

The plan was for the film to be made quickly and cheaply, to try and achieve a high degree of realism. There was the sense that it would be a kind of guerrilla film-making, using amateur actors and real veterans and a budget of around $2 million. Milius had interviewed returning soldiers, some of them his friends, and wove their stories into the narrative of their '**surfing** and bombs' movie. Lucas, entering into the spirit of myth-making that surrounds the film, goes as far as to suggest in ***Hearts of Darkness: A Filmmaker's Apocalypse*** that Milius planned for Lucas and the crew actually to travel to **Vietnam** at the height of the war and shoot the film in the real location. Murch corrects this:

> No, they were planning to make it in the Sacramento Delta, which under certain circumstances has the appearance of the **Mekong** Delta. And it's also the area where George grew up. They were planning to shoot it largely in black and white and largely in 16mm and to make it look like the documentary war films that were coming out and being shown on TV. The approach then was very different to the wide screen high definition lenses that [**Vittorio**] **Storaro** and Francis [Coppola] used.

Apocalypse Now was one of Zoetrope's first projects, the rights for which were bought along with several others by Warner Bros shortly after the establishment of the company in 1969. After the collapse of this deal and the success of *American Graffiti*, Lucas was torn between two projects in different stages of development, a problematic early version of **Star Wars** and the relatively polished *Apocalypse Now*. 1973–4 was a crucial time for the destiny of the film, marking a decisive split between Lucas and the project he had helped to initiate, and in his friendship with Coppola. The reasons for this are not quite clear. Pollock says:

> Lucas was feeling frustrated in his efforts to get *Star Wars* in manageable shape and saw *Apocalypse* as the next logical step in his career. He went to Coppola in early 1973 and said, 'I've got a chance to make this [film], Francis.' But if *Apocalypse* was

to be made, it was with Coppola as producer and owner of 25 percent of the profits, twice as much as Lucas who split his 25 percent with Milius. That didn't seem fair to George, who was still smarting from the profit wrangles over *Graffiti*. 'I couldn't possibly have made the movie under those conditions,' Lucas says, so he turned back to *Star Wars*.

In 1974 Coppola came back to Lucas, trying to persuade him to direct the film, which could come out in 1976, as an ironic contribution to the American bicentennial celebrations. The deal Coppola offered was $25,000 plus 10 per cent of the profits, which seemed to Lucas, and seems still, insulting, especially in view of their friendship and the fact that Lucas was being paid $150,000 to write and direct *Star Wars*. Murch saw it differently – as a reaction to a more general sense of difficulty in getting the project going:

> After that [*American Graffiti*], he still had his sights set on making *Apocalypse Now*, but nobody would budge. The war was still on, or freshly done. It just didn't seem to be a project that people wanted to do. So he sat down and had a long think, 'What was it about Vietnam? What was it about *Apocalypse Now* that I really wanted to make? What was the core story?' So he told the story as *Star Wars*.

On Lucas's rejection of this deal, Coppola decided to direct the film himself, seeing it as a quick, uncomplicated follow-up to the gut-wrenching complexities of *The Godfather Part II*. *Star Wars* was Lucas's third film and, so far, the last he has directed. He has shifted, with enormous commercial success, into production and the development of film technology. Despite the cooling of their friendship, Lucas and Coppola have remained on civil terms, and have collaborated several times, notably on *Mishima: A Life in Four Chapters* and *Tucker: The Man and His Dream*. Lucas's contribution to *Apocalypse Now* was acknowledged by Coppola granting him two profit points, from which he has apparently earnt no money, and the sly naming of the **Harrison Ford** character in **Nha Trang**, **Colonel G. Lucas**.

M

Makavejev, Dusan (b. 1932)

Director born in Belgrade. His films include *WR: Mysteries of the Organism*, *Montenegro* and *The Coca-Cola Kid*. **Coppola** briefly considered him as a possible director for *Apocalypse Now* while still negotiating with **George Lucas**, sending him a copy of the script in Paris, before resolving to direct it himself.

Manson, Charles Milles (b. 1934)

As the **boat** heads on through the strange demilitarised zone after **Do Long bridge** and the crew members go through their new mail, **Chef** reads a letter from his wife or girlfriend which includes a newspaper cutting with a picture of Manson and the partly visible headline:

. . . Doris Day's Son
. . . Slayings in Tate Case

He reads, '"Charles Miller [*sic*] Manson ordered the slaughter of everyone in the house anyway as a sign of protest." That's really weird, ain't it?'

This is one of a quick succession of images that show the **music**, the **drug** culture and the dark side of the late 1960s experience and suggest the proximity of **Kurtz**. While the tape of **Clean**'s mother is played, **Willard** reads about his predecessor **Colby** joining Kurtz, going mad and native, **Lance** talks about **Disneyland** and wafts the

Purple Haze, and Chef reads apparently for the first time about the Manson **Family**. Manson, aka Jesus Christ, God, instigated the ritualistic murders on 10 and 11 August 1969 of seven people, including Roman Polanski's heavily pregnant wife, Sharon Tate.

The house where Tate and four other victims were killed, 10050 Cielo Drive, Los Angeles, was previously owned by Terry Melcher, Doris Day's son. In fact one of the confused murderers was convinced that he still lived there. Melcher had met Manson the previous summer and although he was 'not enthused' by his musical talents, he had hung out with him and Dennis Wilson, the Beach Boys drummer and symbol of drugs, **rock 'n' roll** and **surfing**. Manson has inspired an enduring cult, and here, as always, he is an instantly recognisable embodiment of evil and madness, a charismatic, insane visionary tempted to play God, whose people worship the man and follow every order, however ridiculous.

As a sign of his times, Manson also serves to date the film reasonably accurately. On the assumption that this headline indicates the first time a substantial link (the double link, although he was in no way involved in the crimes) was made between Melcher and the murders, this would put the date of the paper at some time before the beginning of the first Grand Jury hearing (5 December 1969) and around the period when Melcher was interviewed by the Los Angeles police – i.e. the first week of November 1969. According to Colonel William Hokanson (retired), who did two tours of duty in **Vietnam** and Cambodia:

> Mail was handled with the highest priority except in emergency situations. We usually received letters about a week after they were posted in the US – sometimes sooner. It might take two days of processing time in Vietnam once it arrived – one at the postal unit, another in the unit to which you were assigned. Units that moved around a lot, such as the **Air Cavalry**, might have taken an extra day or two.

Therefore the mail would have taken no more than ten days, tops. This would place the action of the film, itself spanning a period of roughly two weeks, some time between mid-November and mid-December 1969. This fits in with the time-scale suggested by the tapes of Kurtz that Willard hears in **Nha Trang**, which were made in December 1968. These were the first documented pieces of his obvious insanity, followed shortly afterwards by his summary execution of the four Vietnamese double agents, leading to the engagement of **Colonel Colby** and, three months later, Willard. The setting of 1969 also coincides with the time when **John Milius** and **George Lucas** began working on the script.

Marcos, Ferdinand (1917–89)

Marcos and his all-singing, all-dancing wife, Imelda, combined the role of oppressive dictator with that of patron of the arts, specifically cinema. For years, until he was deposed, he hosted the annual **Philippines** Film Festival. The Philippines had already been chosen as the preferred location for the production when **George Lucas** was due to direct it. His producer, the appropriately named Gary **Kurtz**, had gone as far as to scout the country for possible locations. It was ideal for the physical similarity of its geography, the cheapness of local labour and the co-operation of its officials. The government lent the production some military **helicopters**, but on 8 April, while the shoot was in Baler, the government withdrew the helicopters to Manila, fearing an attack from the rebels hiding in the nearby hills.

The cheap labour was a crucial factor in allowing the film to happen at all. Hundreds of local workers were employed in the construction of Kurtz's **temple**. This adds an appropriate sense of colonial opportunism in the making of the film, mirroring the background to the war and the circumstances of Belgian imperial exploitation explored in *Heart of Darkness*. In *Notes* **Eleanor Coppola** talks frequently of the problems of money in her and her husband's life in general, and specifically the financial atmosphere surrounding the making of *Apocalypse Now*. **Francis Coppola**, here and elsewhere, risked losing everything, and he has consistently been depicted as a profligate film-maker. Eleanor Coppola seems genuinely indifferent to money and suffered, along with her family, the embarrassment of being and being seen as a millionaire in an impoverished country. Her diary entry for 1 May 1976 notes:

> On Labor Day, President Marcos grants some concessions to the labor movement here. Today's paper says he has raised the minimum wage in Metro Manila to 10 pesos a day, approximately $1.25, and farm labor to 7 pesos a day.

marijuana

The seemingly ubiquitous **drug** of the film appears only a few times. As the boat begins its journey up river, **Lance**, **Clean** and **Chef** share a joint and offer it to **Willard**. He refuses with a barely perceptible shake of the head and closes the curtain on them. They share the stoners' giggle as behind the curtain Willard indulges in his own tipple, replacing the water in his canteen with brandy. At **Hau Phat**, the supply station, Chef says, 'I bet you can score up here,' and asks the Supply Sergeant for some Panama Red. Leaving Hau Phat, just before they pass the rival **PBR**s, Lance passes a joint to Clean and finally, just before they stop the **sampan**, **Chief** loses his temper with the undisciplined stoned bickering of Clean and Chef, reminding Chef that he is in the navy not the army, and ordering him to 'Stop smoking that dope'.

Dope was easily available in **Vietnam**. **Michael Herr** and Tim Page, the photographer, when not witnessing action, seem to have spent much of their time getting stoned with soldiers. A newsreel film from the time has a group of soldiers going down to a water hole at the edge of their camp to, as the commentator puts it, 'turn on with marijuana'. Splendidly, and in what must have appeared to the contemporary viewer a shockingly subversive ritual, they placed the head of a pipe in one end of a gun's barrel and inhaled the smoke from the other. **Francis Coppola** himself began (for the first time in his life) to smoke dope on the set of *Apocalypse Now*.

Marks, Richard (b. 1943)

Editor born in New York City. He worked on, among others, *Little Big Man*, *Serpico* and *The Godfather Part II* before *Apocalypse Now*, on which he oversaw the **editing**, working alongside **Walter Murch** and Gerald Greenberg: 'I'll always remember starting work on the editing. I was living in New York and I flew to San Francisco on January 1st 1977, and worked on it for nearly three years.' The three of them initially tackled the body of the film, from the beginning up to **Kurtz**'s compound, although he explains: 'Over that period of time and in the collaborative, working atmosphere that **Francis** [**Coppola**] creates, you all get to work on everything.'

'The first cut was six or seven hours long and that was without the dossier material, which was shot around that time on location in the Napa Valley,' he says. He took over editing this final sequence from **Dennis Jakob** – 'It was in a confused state, to say the least' – and shaped it into to the relatively concise form in the release version, removing much of the improvisation. He cut the film down, losing what he saw as fine sequences in the process, most notably the **French plantation** scenes. As this process continued and the film emerged in what he describes as an organic process, still 'There was no glue. It lacked the narration and the connective material which was finally added eight or nine months before the film was released.'

Apart from his function as supervisor in the evolution of the film's eventual shape and, in particular, his paring down and simplification of the Kurtz compound sequence, perhaps his finest contribution was the completion of the bracket device. So, after the reprise and conclusion of **'The End'**, as **Willard** and **Lance** head off in the boat, you have the fleeting, ghostly images of a **helicopter**, fire and a **temple** statue, visual echoes of the film's **opening**.

Marks said, 'I look forward to reading your book and reliving the experience of the film, so long as I take a few tranquillisers first.'

Marlow, Charlie

A character in several **Conrad** stories. He is the narrator of *Heart of Darkness*, telling his companions on the *Nellie*, while waiting for the tide on the Thames, the story of his river journey to retrieve the ivory and the wayward and sick **Kurtz**. Conrad's Marlow becomes, or at least has his equivalent in, **Willard**. The change of name, apart from being emblematic of the character, is necessary in a modern film to avoid the confusion of a murder story being accompanied by the cynical, hard-bitten, voice-over narration of a central character called Marlow(e).

Here, as throughout, certain things have changed in transition; for example, Marlow is an experienced seafarer, whereas Willard is an army man on a naval patrol boat, and Marlow is not an **assassin**. *Apocalypse Now* is of course not simply an updated screen version of *Heart of Darkness*, but there are key similarities between the characters. Both are relatively impassive men, who comment on the morality of their actions and surroundings in the narration. Marlow is explicitly Buddha-like, and a Buddha statue appears in Willard's imaginings in the film's opening. Both become fixated on Kurtz as they hear more about his reputation on their respective journeys up river. Both are decisive men of action.

We learn more about Marlow's job as the **caretaker** of Kurtz's memory as he visits Kurtz's fiancée and **lies** to her about Kurtz's **last words**.

Marquand, Christian (b. 1927)

Actor born in Marseilles. He made his debut in a bit part in Cocteau's *La Belle et la béte* (1947) and featured in the 1964 adaptation of **Conrad**'s *Lord Jim*. He plays the head of the family in the **French plantation** sequence, which didn't make it into the final released version of the film.

Mathison, Melissa

Screenwriter (of *E.T.* et al.) married to **Harrison Ford** (**the Colonel**) from 1983. She served as an executive assistant on the film and her unauthorised announcement regarding the state of **Martin Sheen**'s health following his **heart attack** is the 'gossip' that so angers **Coppola**, as seen in *Hearts of Darkness: A Filmmaker's Apocalypse*. Her affair with Coppola on location and afterwards was one of the key factors that threatened to end the Coppolas' marriage. **Eleanor Coppola** refers to this in *Notes*, but doesn't mention Mathison by name.

McQueen, Steve (1930–80)

Actor who became a big star in the 1960s with *The Magnificent Seven*, *The Great Escape*, *Bullitt* and others. McQueen starred in the **Vietnam** allegory *The Sand Pebbles*, the story of a US naval vessel stranded upriver in China in the 1920s. By the mid-1970s he had entered semi-retirement, when **Coppola** nearly persuaded him to accept the role of **Willard**. In the end he decided, like many of those considered for the main roles, that he didn't want to spend (the planned) sixteen weeks in the discomfort of the **jungle** in **the Philippines**. He opted instead for the surprising, small-scale *An Enemy of the People*.

Mekong river

The river up which **Marlow** travels in order to confront **Kurtz** is never referred to by name, but it is very clearly intended to be the

Congo – from Marlow's description of it snaking through the centre of the map he first saw as a child (**Conrad**'s own childhood memory) and based on Conrad's experiences described in his *Congo Diary*. In the same way, the river in *Apocalypse Now*, referred to as the **Nung river**, is an invention that obviously is supposed to be seen as the Mekong.

Willard is taken by helicopter from **Nha Trang**, presumably south along the coast, where he joins the crew of the naval patrol boat. The boat skirts the coastline before meeting (prematurely) the **Air Cavalry**. The point they choose to join the river is one of several possibilities, like the Mekong itself, with its various branches into the sea. It snakes through **Vietnam** before flowing into (and through) Cambodia.

Various inconsistencies have been pointed out regarding *Apocalypse Now*'s presumed geographical setting. The **surfing** is more likely to happen in central than southern Vietnam, where the Nung/Mekong meets the sea. Also the real Mekong flows largely through paddy fields, not **jungle**. Should we simply put this down to expediency and artistic licence?

method

A thread running through the film is the balance between method and madness, the requirements of 'practical military necessity' in contrast to pointless, random acts of brutality. The absurdly genteel, ironic understatement that **Kurtz** is being relieved of his station/terminated because of his unsound methods is central to both *Heart of Darkness* and *Apocalypse Now*. As **Marlow** recalls his approach to the Inner Station, he tells his listeners, 'In fact the Manager said afterwards that Mr Kurtz's methods had ruined the district.' Later, having surveyed the station and seen the impaled **heads** of the 'rebels', the Manager says to Marlow that Kurtz has done more harm than good:

'"Because the method is unsound." "Do you," said I looking

at the shore, "call it 'unsound method'?" "Without doubt,"
he exclaimed hotly. "Don't you?" . . . "No method at all," I
murmured after a while.'

In *Apocalypse Now*, when **Willard** receives his mission in **Nha Trang
the General** tells him that Kurtz joined the Special Forces and 'after
that his ideas, his methods became unsound. Unsound.' When Willard
confronts Kurtz, Kurtz asks him:

'What did they tell you?'
    'They told me that you had gone totally insane and, er, that
your methods were unsound.'
    'Are my methods unsound?'
    [pause, then flatly] 'I don't see [pause] any method [pause] at
all.'

This last stiltedly delivered response is the film's strangest and most
haunting line, echoing **Conrad** and reflecting Willard's shock and
incomprehension at coming face to face with Kurtz, the representative
of madness, his own dark side, and that of the **Vietnam War** and
America itself. The already quiet Willard is rendered nearly dumb
by the revelation of what is at the end of his quest, what is at the
heart of darkness. The line is lent a further incidental piquancy by
being delivered by one trainee in 'the method' to its most famous
exponent.

Apocalypse Now has become one medium through which people
see the Vietnam War. Oliver Stone's authentic evocation of his own
experiences as an infantry private in the war, shown in *Platoon*, would
seem to have been filtered through the cinematic template of the
war in *Apocalypse Now*. In a similar way Clark Clifford, Robert
McNamara's successor as head of the US Defense Department, appears
to have been influenced by the language of the film. Talking to
Stanley Karnow in 1981 he assessed America's intentions in **Vietnam**:

'We felt that we were doing what was necessary. It proved to be unsound.'

Milius, John (b. 1944)

Writer-director born in St Louis. He studied English at Los Angeles City College and was rejected by the Marines because of his chronic asthma. He attended University of Southern California Film School, from where he graduated, like his own mentor **Coppola**, to the informal academy of Roger Corman's American International Pictures. The films with which he is associated as writer, director or producer have strong unifying themes. If you look at *Dirty Harry*, *The Life and Times of Judge Roy Bean*, *Jeremiah Johnson*, *Magnum Force*, *Dillinger*, *The Wind and the Lion*, **Big Wednesday**, *Apocalypse Now*, *Conan the Barbarian*, *Uncommon Valor* and *Farewell to the King*, you see that they share certain signature Milius themes: transcendence from human to mythical stature, uncompromising violence, a right-wing sensibility in which self-reliant heroes and anti-heroes flout rules to do what they see as just. John Milius has seen *The Seven Samurai* fifty times. *Of Apocalypse Now* Milius recalls proudly (and typically adopting military language), 'I was ten years on that film. I was the longest employee on *Apocalypse Now*. I had the longest tour of duty.' When asked how well the finished film reflects his own conception of the project, he concludes, 'Pretty darn well.' He wrote the first of his ten drafts for *Apocalypse Now* initially to redress the balance in favour of the decent, hard-done-by American soldier in **Vietnam** exemplified by **Robert Rheault**. He saw that **Heart of Darkness** lent itself in several ways to the story of the war, but:

> It was never intended to be real close to the book at all. I didn't even read the book again. I had read it when I was seventeen. When I wrote the screenplay I didn't re-read it because I almost felt that I had dreamt the book. I wasn't sure that what I remembered – some of the things that I remembered

from the story – really was there. I didn't want to go back and find out that they weren't really there. **George Lucas** had never read *Heart of Darkness*, in fact neither had Francis.

Asked how much George Lucas contributed to the script, he replies simply, 'Nothing – other than just saying, "Let's do a movie in Vietnam."'

During the shoot, Milius was invited to the location on a number of occasions, but every time

Francis would say 'Don't come.' I found out later that the reason he didn't want me to come was that he was afraid there would be a coup. Because they thought he was crazy, and if I came, a qualified director who certainly knew the story, they could throw a net over him. And a straight-jacket. Not that I would foment a coup. That would be the last thing I would do. He was my Führer. He is, he's the Führer, a great charismatic leader. There was no doubt, from the moment he stepped in that he would make a much better film than either George or I would have.

Milius often refers to Coppola as his Führer, or even Hitler, and it is meant as a compliment. In *Hearts of Darkness: A Filmmaker's Apocalypse* Milius remembers his recall to the project when Coppola convinced him it would be the first film to win the Nobel Peace Prize. This was when the film was being cut, and he was brought in 'Just to put things in order, have things make sense, work out why things were the way they were'. He concludes his memories of the film thus:

There were good and bad things about the experience. But I always remember the wonderful ambition of the project, the idea that Francis brought to it that 'We can really do something great, whatever the cost.' He was hard on himself, worrying that what he was doing was **pretentious**, but he was going for greatness. He had to have a kind of hubris to get away with doing this kind of film. He always had these very lofty ambitions and I don't recall ever hearing that from anybody else, or being influenced that way. David Lean was like that. They would seem insane at times, but that's what you should try and do when you make a movie.

Montagnards

By the time **Willard** gets his mission, as **the Colonel** explains, **Kurtz** has moved across the border into Cambodia with his utterly dedicated Montagnard army. The Montagnards are indigenous mountain-dwelling people in North and South **Vietnam**. The realism of the film has been criticised in this aspect as the Montagnards seem to have been recruited from the area of the supposed **Mekong river** around the border between Vietnam and Cambodia, where there are no mountains. This may be a small error, but then again Kurtz may have gone to a mountainous region to round up his army. It's not exactly Spartacus wearing a Rolex, or Cleopatra riding pillion on a Ducati.

Michael Herr writes in *Dispatches*:

Because the Highlands of Vietnam are spooky, unbelievably spooky, spooky beyond belief. They are a run of erratic mountain ranges, gnarled valleys, jungled ravines and abrupt plains where Montagnard villages cluster, thin and disappear as the terrain steepens. The Montagnards in all of their tribal components make up the most primitive and mysterious portion of the Vietnamese population, a population that has always confused Americans even in its most Westernized segments. Strictly speaking, the Montagnards are not Vietnamese at all, certainly not *South* Vietnamese, but a kind of upgraded, demi-enlightened Annamese aborigine, often living in nakedness and brooding silence in their villages. Most Vietnamese and most Montagnards considered each other inferior, and while many Montagnards hired out as mercenaries to the Special Forces, that older, racially based enmity often slowed down the allied effort. Many Americans considered them to be nomadic, but the war had more to do with that than anything in their temperament. We napalmed off their crops and flattened their villages, and then admired the restlessness in their spirit. Their nakedness, their painted bodies, their recalcitrance, their silent composure before strangers, their benign savagery, and the sheer awesome ugliness of them combined to make most Americans who were forced to associate with them a little uncomfortable over the long run.

Murch, Walter

Sound designer, sound editor, editor, writer and director born in New York City and employed on *Apocalypse Now* in the first four of these capacities. UCLA Film School spawned **Coppola**, Carroll Ballard, **Dennis Jakob** and Jim Morrison. Around the same time, Walter Murch, **John Milius** and **George Lucas** were across town attending USC. These people (minus Morrison, of course) moved into Hollywood in Coppola's wake, forming the core of the group that became American **Zoetrope**. Murch has worked extensively with Coppola and Lucas in different roles; he was responsible for the sound on *The Rain People*, *THX 1138* (for which he also co-wrote the script), *American Graffiti*, *The Conversation* (also co-editor) and *The Godfather Part II*. He worked uncredited on *The Godfather*. He edited Coppola's *The Godfather Part III*, as well as, among others, *Julia*, *Ghost* and *The English Patient* (for which he won an Oscar).

During the break in filming as the storms were wrecking the sets on the **Philippine** locations, Coppola returned to San Francisco, where he and Murch spent a couple of weeks polishing the script. Murch remembers, 'We worked on the **sampan** scene, the scene where the canopy catches fire. Anything where there's contact between the boat and the river.' After this he went to London to work on *Julia* (which subsequently earnt him an Oscar nomination).

> I didn't come on to the film until the Summer of '77. Francis had come back from the Philippines through London. We had gone out to dinner and he had talked to me earlier about doing the sound for the film. I agreed to do it, so I came back and expected the film to be ready to do the sound. At that time the film was supposed to come out in December of '77, which was very shortly. But when I arrived it was clear that the film wasn't anywhere near being finished. So there was a period of adjustment of two or three weeks where Francis had to admit that it was going to have to be postponed until around Easter '78, which was still quite close. It meant that a lot of the other work had to get done, so I started **editing** the picture, just to try to help get it done, and I joined **Richie Marks** and Gerry Greenberg, and Dennis Jakob, who was assigned to **the end** of the film.

Murch worked on the editing, the **sound design** and sound editing, employing his own **quadrophonic/quintaphonic** sound, recording authentic sounds for the film's **weapons**, overseeing the shooting of the dossier material.

He scored one of *Apocalypse Now*'s two **Academy Award** successes, sharing the Oscar for Best Sound with Mark Berger, Nat Boxer and Richard Beggs.

music

See **soundtrack**.

My Lai

See **sampan**; **Robert Rheault**.

Trees, like palm trees in the distance, fill up the foreground. They hardly move, maybe the tops are swaying a bit, the sky behind is dull and pale blue. A wispy bit of cloud floats across the bottom. A slow rotating sound from somewhere else gets louder but still sounds distant as a heavy looking grey copter moves across the sky in front of the trees. It moves slowly but is gone quickly. Some yellow dust floats up in the wind and follows behind it, then fades back into the green. There's some music, just strobing away, about to get to something. A bit more yellow dust smokes up, leaving a huge silence behind it. Then the music kicks in. Nothing happens but dust. Then the trees behind turn the dust green, you can only see their tops. The rotor sound fades in again, another copter flies higher up this time, you can only see the bottom rails. It's passed, leaving the same misted-out background. So quietly, silently, three fires flare up into the trees. They roll upwards, blinding orange, then three more explode, one, two... three. They roll into one ginormous billowing ball, it's so huge, it's everything. Then it disappears into its own smoke, deep, murky, impenetrable, poisonous green. Just a small fleck of orange flame shows through. The music, it's singing, comes through too, it's all slow and building, "...this is the end...", it's like the first time. It's so deep, all that smoky green. The green copters float past, left to right, right to left, like shadows. The scene sort of slips past, but doesn't change much. The fire gets tugged off in the copters' wind. The picture fades into murky colours, it's impossible to work out what's what. Everything's sort of revealing itself, slowly – it's the slowest. Gradually, in the end, a face comes through. Both eyes stare straight ahead, just looking out at you. I can't tell the face cos it's upside down, but the music's getting hotter and the face is hot too. Something whirrs inconspicuously in in front of it. The eyes blink, and I think they flick left. The background still passes behind, faded out behind the face. More copters, big, faded ones.

The eyes definitely look left and then right, blinking more, the face is totally expressionless, the landscape fires up, it's unclear what's upside down now. The fire's intense. The face is moving. A hand appears in front of it and he drags on a cigarette, still staring straight out – or up. The trees, burnt black as anything, move off. The fire moves with them. The face is still there, shining with sweat. Stuff falls from what's left of the trees, really slowly, it's black and just floats down behind the face. The fire has nothing left to burn but it burns on anyway, so orange. He takes another drag. The whole picture fades out, apart from one raging fire in the middle. A helicopter flies in from the left then another from the right, they cross right in the middle. A fan whirrs round on the ceiling, beating time with the copter blades. You can see the man's shoulders. His body moves round so he's not upside down anymore, and then there are some letters and a photograph strewn across the table at the side of the bed. The bright orange fire bores through it all, just a small bit in the corner, but it's more important than everything else – even though it's just a dream of somewhere else. He lies next to all of this gear, and there's an empty glass, his left hand holds a burnt-out cigarette, the fan blades beat louder. All that stuff from behind, the palm trees and fire, are back again – across everything, and it's not the fan at all, it's helicopters beating. There's a pistol on the sheet next to him. He blinks up at the fan then across the room at the window, masked off by the venetian blinds. It's all orange, but a different hazy orange. You see him differently, his mouth moves, but definitely unconsciously. Then the blinds get closer and closer, so they get out of focus, he flicks them apart and takes a peek out. It's a street, cars, things moving quickly, some trees. A slat of light lines his face and you see him like a man for the first time. A voice comes over, slow and deep, "Saigon, shiiitt!" You know it's his voice. He moves his head back a bit and slugs something from a glass. He holds it in his mouth then

N

Nam, The

An exhibition of and accompanying book (1996/7) of 'still films' by Fiona Banner inspired by the idea that 'the power of images has long replaced the force of the written word'. She has transcribed **Vietnam War Films** – *Apocalypse Now, Born on the Fourth of July, Full Metal Jacket, Hamburger Hill, Platoon* and *Full Metal Jacket* – on to canvases and subsequently the pages of a book, turning them into 'wordscapes'.

napalm

A mixture of gasoline, naphthenic and palmatic acids – it is projected on to targets from flame throwers or in bombs. It was developed by Dow Chemical Inc. and first used in the Korean War. Philip Jones Griffiths, in *Vietnam Inc.,* describes it as 'the most effective "anti personnel" weapon'. He recalls a pilot explaining to him in 1968:

> We sure are pleased with those backroom boys at Dow. The original product wasn't so hot – if the **gooks** were quick they could scrape it off. So the boys started adding polystyrene – now it sticks like shit to a blanket. But then if the gooks jumped under water it stopped burning, so they started adding Willie Peter [WP – white phosphorous] so's to make it burn better. It'll even burn under water now. And just one drop is enough, it'll keep burning right down to the bone so they die anyway from phosphorous poisoning.

'Never get out of the boat'

Chef repeats this line hysterically after his encounter with the **tiger**, and **Willard** takes it up in his narration: 'Never get out of the boat. Absolutely god damn right. Not unless you were going all the way . . . **Kurtz** got off the boat.' This is a statement about America's involvement in **Vietnam**. It was a war of time in which one side would have to run out of it eventually, a battle of wills where one side was motivated by self-determination, the other by its irrational but powerful fear of the domino effect of a communist victory in South-east Asia. The time element is crucial, because America's involvement was literally based on the impermanence of its presence in South Vietnam. The US attempted, by aligning itself with the increasingly feeble South Vietnamese army and sponsoring a succession of corrupt and ineffectual puppet emperors, to establish a system which would remain after the inevitable US withdrawal. Jonathan Schell sums up the central flaws neatly in *The Real War*:

> The war must be prolonged, and we must have time. Time is on our side – time will be our best strategist, if we are determined to pursue our resistance to the end.
> (Truong Chinh, Secretary General of the Communist Party of Vietnam, spring, 1947)

> We ran out of time. This is the tragedy of Vietnam – we were fighting for time rather than space. And time ran out.
> (Norman B. Hannah, Foreign Service officer with experience in Vietnam, 1975)

The puzzle of how the world's mightiest power was defeated by a tiny weak one begins to melt away once the principle enunciated by Truong Chinh in 1947 and reaffirmed, twenty-eight years and millions of lives later, by Norman B. Hannah is entered into the equation. Success in the war for space – the capture of this or that Hamburger Hill – meant nothing if, when it was all over and the Americans withdrew, the balance of Vietnamese forces was left unchanged from what it had been when the United States arrived.

A tactical system emerged from or existed within the bewildering mess of the war which was predicated on America's eventual withdrawal. The American military plan was criticised in Vietnam for the same reasons that it would be in the Gulf War and its aftermath. There was an insufficient use of expertise in the area. The might of America moved to South-east Asia, bringing its cultural trappings along. To expose yourself to the country, the **jungle**, is to risk danger, to risk going native. The boat, a microcosm of America manned by a cross-section of American soldiers, chugs through a nightmare of madness and ever-increasing hostility. It represents a desperate buffer against foreign influence. Here, as elsewhere, the film takes on the shape and mood of a horror film, with the occupants not realising that the boat is being sucked inexorably up river towards Kurtz and the heart of darkness and that it (with the leaves replacing the burnt canopy) and they (with the **water burial** of **Chief** and the excised land burial of **Clean**) are literally being swallowed up by the river and jungle.

Nha Trang

Town on west coast of **Vietnam** and the site of US intelligence headquarters in II Corps. **Willard** is escorted to his meeting there from his hotel in **Saigon**. Here Willard meets **the General**, **the Colonel** and the civilian – the men with no name (except **Corman**, **Lucas** and **Jerry**) – who introduce him by photo and tape to his quarry over a little lunch. This is an unsettling scene, with anonymous people, an air of nervousness, with pauses, stammering and awkward swallowing – while speaking that is, as little food is seen to be eaten. The beef, which is not bad, is accompanied by peas, carrots and bread rolls. Finally, the dodgy **shrimp** – all washed down with iced tea. Significantly, the shrimp are sampled only by the civilian, who also carves the beef on his plate while the General gives Willard some background information on **Kurtz**. To be shown eating – in fact to be seen consuming anything more substantial than a cup of black coffee – in a film is often to be signalled as a weak or shifty character.

Food, particularly the details of its preparation, play a serious role in **Coppola**'s work. There is the famous scene in *The Godfather*, in which Fat Clemenza initiates Michael in the ways of perfect spaghetti sauce. In fact, a thesis could be written on the use of citrus fruit in that film. With the removal of the **French plantation** sequence, this marks the only chance for Coppola to flex his foody muscles in *Apocalypse Now*.

Discussing Louis Malle's *My Dinner With André*, Robert Zemeckis says: 'Remember that scene in *Apocalypse Now* when they're eating? Great set-ups! More angles in that than in the rest of the film – cutting the shrimp and passing the meat. Wow!'

Nicholson, Jack (b. 1937)

Actor born in New Jersey. Star of *Easy Rider*, *Five Easy Pieces*, *Chinatown*, *One Flew Over the Cuckoo's Nest*, *The Shining*, *The Witches of Eastwick* and *As Good as it Gets*, among many others. He was an early choice of **Coppola**'s to play **Kurtz** and you can imagine how he, unlike many other possible actors, could have been interesting if not enigmatic in the part. **Marlon Brando** whispers and simmers in a way that makes you think of him as a once great man, now a spent force. Jack Nicholson enjoys the roles of madness and evil too obviously, and his quiet moments tend to be preludes to an eruption. In *A Few Good Men* Nicholson played a fierce, disciplinarian Marine colonel covering up the violence of his subordinates.

What-if games may be pointless, but, as great as the film is, it is tempting to imagine an alternative version starring, say, **Al Pacino** or

Steve McQueen as **Willard**, **Gene Hackman** as **Kilgore** and Jack Nicholson as Kurtz. It could have been equally fascinating.

nirvana now

The chief inspiration for the film's title. **Milius** named his film project in ironic counterpoint to a popular flower power badge of the late 1960s bearing this motto.

Nixon, Richard M. (1913–1994)

In the **Playboy Bunnies** scene, as well as suggesting the famous pictures of the fall of **Saigon** with soldiers clinging on desperately to the departing **helicopter**, **Bill Graham** evokes President Nixon, according to Paul Cullum at least. His 'craven exit is marked by a shyster shrug, the famous V for Victory wave and tear gas [*sic*] canisters, suggesting Nixon three times over'. Thus the film completes its references to the triumvirate, albeit somewhat tentatively in each case, of American presidents responsible for the official entry into, escalation in and final withdrawal from **Vietnam**.

Notes

Eleanor Coppola's diaries covering the years of the film's production. The book is in part an insight into life with a very stressed genius director, and life on and around a film set. So you do learn a lot about the inside world of film-making. But it is at least as much about the breakdown of a marriage. This was to some degree a result of the anxiety **Francis Coppola** suffered during the shooting. He was working on a film that was apparently incoherent, that had no ending, that suffered the replacement of the star early on, that endured the whims of its huge cameo star, that was subject to the vicissitudes of the **Philippine** airforce and weather, in which Coppola was personally investing much of his newly acquired wealth, and he seemed continually in danger of losing himself in hyper-empathy for any one of the film's dangerously insane central characters.

So the book is an absorbing journey through this experience, a litany of near and actual disaster, and Eleanor Coppola seems to have been remarkably supportive through all these trials, especially as she was herself looking after their young family and directing a documentary on the film's making, the footage for which eventually surfaced in *Hearts of Darkness: A Filmmaker's Apocalypse*. She seems genuinely not to have cared that her husband was daily risking her family's livelihood. The most overwhelming of their marital problems was simply her husband's infidelity. Coppola was serially unfaithful during the shoot, his most serious affair being with **Melissa Mathison**. Although no one is mentioned by name in Eleanor Coppola's diaries, she is frank in recounting the devastation that these liaisons caused her.

She emerges from the book as sympathetic but somehow sad, living in the shadow of a driven egomaniac, unable to find her own role, frustrated by her own lack of focus, always embarking on and then abandoning new artistic endeavours. Barring her repeated references to the I Ching, this is a valuable look at the gloomy side of a Hollywood marriage and an invaluable aid to all *Apocalypse Now* fans.

Nung river

The fictional river up which the **PBR** travels, clearly intended to be the **Mekong river**. The Nung are a Vietnamese ethnic group of the Tay-Thai language group.

O

Odyssey, The

Homer's epic poem describes the ten-year journey of the Greek hero Odysseus back from the defeat of Troy to his home of Ithaca. It is one of the oldest surviving narratives, a succession of adventures and trials, and it is cited by **John Milius** as one of the primary sources for his original script. In *Hearts of Darkness: A Filmmaker's Apocalypse* he mentions this source and elaborates by drawing a parallel between **Kilgore** and the Cyclops Polyphemus. This bears a little examination as Odysseus and his men escape from the Cyclops by getting him drunk, blinding him with a pole sharpened in a camp-fire, and clinging on to the undersides of his sheep as they leave his island cave. Polyphemus, suspecting the plot, asks who is there and Odysseus (who had introduced himself as 'No one') replies 'No one' and this is enough to fool the big dumb idiot. Likewise, Kilgore is persuaded to take the boat to the mouth of the **Nung river**, after drinking around the camp-fire, by the coincidence of it offering a fantastic peak. Well, maybe likewise-ish.

Similarly, Milius likens the **Playboy Bunnies** to the Sirens, who sing so beautifully that they tempt sailors towards them to their doom on treacherous rocks and against whose charms Odysseus blocks his ears. The similarity becomes a little flimsy in the release version of the film. The Bunnies as temptresses theme was explored further in longer, early cuts when the **PBR** encountered them again further up the river from **Hau Phat**. The **helicopter** carrying the agent and the Bunnies has run out of fuel and **Willard** arranges to supply them with some in exchange for the crew spending twenty minutes each with the **women**. One could continue and try to establish hidden links between the lost **French plantation** sequence and the Lotus-Eaters and Circe, but again this is taking the film too literally and the playful Milius too seriously. What it points to is the intention and the ambition of the project from the outset – to place the story of the film within a framework of mythology and storytelling beginning with Homer, Virgil and **the Bible**, and leading up to **Conrad** and **Eliot** in the twentieth century.

Ohio river

One of the many rivers that flow through the story of the film. **Willard** tells **Kurtz** that he was born about 200 miles away from the river that Kurtz himself travelled down as a child when he saw heaven fall to earth in the form of **gardenias**. **Martin Sheen** was born in Dayton, Ohio, about fifty miles from the Ohio river.

P

PBR

Patrol boat river. Called *Erebus*.

> I was being ferried down the coast in a Navy PBR, a type of plastic patrol boat, a pretty common sight on the rivers.

The fact that the journey puts a regular army man in a navy boat is not overplayed but, especially in the strained relationship between **Willard** and **Chief**, is representative of the internecine conflicts within the American forces in **Vietnam**. **Michael Herr**, in *Dispatches*, makes a lot of the rivalry among the **Air Cavalry**, the Marines and the army:

> There was a week in the war, one week, when the Army lost more men killed, proportionately, than the Marines, and Army spokesmen had a rough time hiding their pride, their absolute glee.

Later, he recalls a story about:

> a marine who had been staked to a hillside by the NVA [North Vietnamese Army]: Marine choppers refused to pick him up, so the Cav went down and got him. Whether it was true or not, it revealed the complexities of the Marine–Cav rivalry, and when the Cav sent an outfit to relieve the Marines on [hill] 471, it

killed off one of the last surviving romances about war left from
the movies: there was no shouting, no hard kidding, no gleeful
obscenities, or the old 'Hey, where you from? Brooklyn? No
kiddin'! Me too!' The departing and arriving files passed one
another without a single word.

There are many points at which the film's plausibility and verisi-
militude have been called into question: the flexible geography of
the locations regarding the river and **surfing**, the **Montagnards**
coming from a mountainless area, the use of what is patently not
live ammunition, and so on. These tend to be either trivial, pedantic
quibbles or genuinely explicable. The use of the boat is a fundamental
requisite of the plot, which requires, like its partial source in *Heart of
Darkness*, the gradual emergence of **Kurtz**'s character, a slow passage
through a series of adventures. But to allow this structure initially seems
to require a narrative sleight of hand, the counter-intuitive logic of a
horror movie. As Colonel Hokanson points out:

> From a military standpoint, sending a single patrol boat up the
> river was an absurd mission. It could accomplish no military
> purpose and could be easily ambushed and sunk by a squad armed
> with RPGs (Soviet rocket-propelled grenades) or with mines, or
> with any number of other readily available means. The trip up the
> river makes no sense except as an updated version of **Conrad**.

The film-makers are of course aware of this problem and **Willard**'s
narration attempts to dismiss this hastily:

> They said it was a good way to pick up information and move
> without drawing a lot of attention. That was OK. I needed the
> air and the time.

During the two weeks of rewrites while **the Philippines** set was
being rebuilt after the hurricanes, **Walter Murch** fleshed out the

boat's role, adding the scenes of the canopy catching fire and the **sampan** massacre:

> At the point when I read the script, the problem I saw with it was that the boat glided up the river without having any contact with either side. It was as if they were on a magic carpet. Another job of the PBR was as a police boat, to stop suspicious boats, so I thought it would be a good idea to have a moment where the PBR actually did what it was supposed to do rather than just be a taxi to carry Willard upriver.

The boat has the radio code-name Street Gang.

Pacino, Al (b. 1940)

Actor born in New York City. Throughout his career he has moved between stage and screen. He became an international film star under the direction of **Coppola** in *The Godfather* films. Coppola fought for two casting decisions in particular, the two central roles, **Marlon Brando** as Vito Corleone and Al Pacino as his educated war-hero son Michael, who cannot escape his destiny and is drawn into the family business. Coppola wanted to repeat this inspired casting coup in *Apocalypse Now*, hoping that Pacino would play **Willard**. As Peter Cowie writes in *Coppola*, Pacino was 'concerned about the long absence from the United States, and feared falling ill in the **jungle** as he had done in the Dominican Republic during the shooting of *The Godfather Part II*'.

You can imagine Pacino being very effective in the role, certainly more appropriate than **Harvey Keitel**, but you can't quite see him pulling off the stillness and impassivity that is so central to the characterisation by **Sheen**. Also, coming straight off the Corleone saga, this recognised cinematic relationship between Pacino and Brando would have overstated the implicit father–son relationship between Willard and **Kurtz**. Pacino later played a retired army officer, the blind colonel in *Scent of a Woman*.

paddy water

When **Willard** first encounters **Kilgore**, after he has distributed the **death cards**, he notices a wounded **Viet Cong** soldier being watched over by an American and two South Vietnamese soldiers. He approaches them:

KILGORE: Hey, what's this? What is this?

AMERICAN SOLDIER: This man's hurt pretty bad, sir. About the only thing holding his guts in is that pot lid.

KILGORE: Yeah, what did he have to say?

SOUTH VIETNAMESE SOLDIER: This soldier is dirty VC. He wants water. He can drink paddy water.

KILGORE, pushing the South Vietnamese Soldier away: Get out of here. [To his aide] Gimme that, gimme that canteen.

SVS: Dirty VC.

KILGORE: Any man brave enough to . . .

SVS, obstructing him: He's killing a lot of our people.

KILGORE: Get out of here or I'll kick your fucking ass. Any man brave enough to fight with his guts strapped can drink from my canteen any day. [He is instantly distracted by the news that one of the **PBR** crew is **Lance Johnson**, the surfer.]

This episode is lifted directly form the account of the photographer and later president of Magnum, Philip Jones Griffiths. His 1971 book of photoreportage, *Vietnam Inc.*, features a photograph of two American GIs and a South Vietnamese soldier crouching over a badly wounded VC soldier, with the caption:

WOUNDED VIETCONG . . . GIs often show a compassion for the enemy that springs from admiration of their dedication and bravery. This VC had a three-day-old stomach wound. He'd picked up his intestines and put them in an enamel bowl (borrowed from a surprised farmer's wife) and strapped it around his middle. As he was being carried to the headquarters company for interrogation, he indicated he was thirsty. 'OK, him VC, him drink dirty water,' said the Vietnamese interpreter, pointing to the brown paddy-field. With real anger a GI told him to keep quiet, then mumbled, 'Any soldier who can fight for three days with his insides out can drink from my canteen any time!'

Philippines, the

The Philippines seemed the ideal location for the film for a variety of reasons, almost all of which backfired. It had already seemed the perfect stand-in for **Vietnam** when **George Lucas** planned to direct the film, and his producer Gary Kurtz had made a couple of recces for precise locations before he left the project to pursue *Star Wars*. **Eleanor Coppola** explains in *Notes*:

> The Philippines was chosen as the location because of the similarity of the terrain to Vietnam, the fact that the Philippine Government was willing to rent its American made **helicopters** and military equipment to the production and that building and labor costs were generally low.

The production became some kind of approximation of the war – mad, shapeless and hugely expensive. The original set of **Hau Phat**, although relatively cheaply built, was not equal to the unpredictable monsoon storms of May 1976 and had to be rebuilt, delaying the production, at great cost. Also it wasn't foreseen that an administration (headed by a leader known to be corrupt and ruthless) so willingly bought might prove to be inefficient and unreliable. The **Marcos** regime faced continual rebellions and, as has often been reported, the helicopters used in the film were several times called away to quell resistance in the nearby mountains, sometimes in the middle of shots.

Eleanor Coppola's entry for 5 May 1976 reports:

All day yesterday, the Philippine Air Force general was on the set with some ladies in sundresses, sitting in the director's chairs, as if he had come to a spectator sport. The production is paying a fortune to rent the helicopters, and every day they send different pilots who don't understand the directions or who weren't flying during the rehearsal the day before. They don't fly in the right place, and wreck thousands and thousands of dollars' worth of shots. The helicopters flown by inexperienced pilots shows in the footage. American pilots just don't fly like that.

The prospect of a difficult, physically uncomfortable location shoot helped to shape the film, acting as a sufficient deterrent for many of those initially approached to appear in it, notably **Al Pacino**, **Steve McQueen** and **Jack Nicholson**. Yet it emerged as the perfect location, with the violent weather, the unco-operative pilots, the whole atmosphere and look that seep on to the screen, helping to create the film itself and contributing to the equally important surrounding mythology.

photo-journalist, the

Coppola initially intended to cast **Dennis Hopper** as a **Green Beret** sidekick to **Kurtz**, but hearing him jabber away on set realised that he would be perfect as an updated version of **Conrad**'s Russian trader/harlequin. It would have been quite conceivable for a photographer to have made it into Cambodia at this time. Photographers received special accreditation and were able to travel relatively freely and safely. It being Dennis Hopper, it is impossible not to see the character in *Apocalypse Now* as a kind of extension of his druggy, paranoid biker from *Easy Rider*.

Equally, as a composite role, you can see elements of other emblematic characters there. Certainly he is reminiscent in his craziness and his looks of **Charles Manson**, about whom **Chef** reads on the **PBR**.

Hopper knew several of **the Family**'s victims and in his compulsion to understand the crimes he visited Manson in jail. He is also clearly partly based upon Tim Page, the eccentric English photographer, companion of **Michael Herr** and Sean Flynn. Page smoked a lot of **dope** (and left a bit of his brain) in **Vietnam**. But these similarities and his habit of quoting **Eliot** apart, he is the character most like his equivalent in *Heart of Darkness*. He has a funny appearance and rattles away 'as if making up for lots of silence'. As the boat pulls up to Kurtz's compound Chef/the Manager shouts out about his fears, having already been attacked. The photographer shouts back:

Apocalypse Now	*Heart of Darkness*
'It's all right. It's all right. It's all been approved.' 'Zap 'em with your siren, man. Zap 'em with your siren.'	'It's all right. Come along. It's all right.' In the next breath he advised me to keep enough steam in the boiler: 'One good screech will do more for you than all your rifles.'
'There's mines over there. There's mines over there too.'	'Look out, Captain!' he cried; 'there's a snag lodged in here last night.'

He establishes citizenship

'I'm an American, American civilian. Hi, Yanks.'	'Brother sailor . . .'
'You got the cigarettes and that's what I've been dreaming of.'	'What! Tobacco! English tobacco, the excellent English tobacco. Now that's brotherly. Smoke!'

He explains that he is well travelled

'Well, poowee. Poowee,
baby. I'll tell you one thing.
this boat is a mess, man.
Whew.'

'My faith, your pilot-house
wants a clean-up.'

WILLARD: 'Who are these
people?'
PHOTO-JOURNALIST: 'Yeah,
well. They think you've come
to take him away.'

'Why did they attack us?' I
pursued.
He hesitated, then said
shamefacedly, 'They don't
want him to go.'

WILLARD: 'Could we talk to
Colonel Kurtz?'
P-J: 'You don't talk to the
Colonel. You, er, listen to
him.'

'Don't you talk with Colonel
Kurtz?' I said.
'You don't talk with
that man – you listen
to him,' he exclaimed with
severe exaltation

'He's enlarged my mind.'

'I tell you,' he cried, 'this man
has enlarged my mind.'

'I'm a little man. I'm a little
man. He's a great man.'

'I! I! I'm a simple man. . . .
How can you compare me
to . . . ?'

'He can be terrible.'

'He could be very terrible.'

P-J: 'I can tell you something
like the other day, he wanted
to kill me, or something like
that.'
WILLARD: 'Why did he want
to kill you?'
P-J: 'Because I took his picture.

'Now – just to give you an
idea – I don't mind telling
you, he wanted to shoot me
too one day – but I don't judge
him.' 'Shoot you!' I cried.
'What for?' 'Well, I had a small
lot of ivory . . . he wanted it

He said, 'If you take my picture again, I'm gonna kill you.' And he meant it.'

and wouldn't hear reason. He declared he would shoot me unless I gave him the ivory and cleared out of the country, because he could do so, and had a fancy for it, and there was nothing on earth to prevent him from killing whom he jolly well pleased.'

'He gets friendly again, he really does.'

'I had to be careful for a time, till we got friendly again for a time

'But you don't judge the Colonel. You don't judge the Colonel like an ordinary man.'

'You can't judge Mr Kurtz as you would an ordinary man.'

'The **heads**. You're looking at the heads. Sometimes he goes too far. He's the first to admit it.'

'The admirer of Mr Kurtz was a bit crestfallen. In a hurried, indistinct voice he began to assure me that he had not dared to take these – say, symbols – down.'

CHEF: 'He's gone crazy.'
P-J: 'Wrong! Wrong! If you could have heard the man just two days ago. If you had heard him then. You were gonna call him crazy?'

'Why! He's mad,' I said. He protested indignantly. Mr Kurtz couldn't be mad. If I had heard him talk only two days ago I wouldn't dare hint at such a thing.

'He forgets himself with his people. Forgets him*self*.'

'[He would] disappear for weeks – forget himself amongst these people   forget himself – you know.'

After Willard's first encounter with Kurtz he is locked in the bamboo cage, and the photo-journalist circles him, launching into a strange, speedy speech, the gist of which is that Kurtz is dying, but that he has mysterious plans for Willard. 'He's got plans for you,' says the photographer, while **Conrad**'s Kurtz tells **Marlow** that 'I had immense plans.' In the film these plans turn out to be for Willard to explain his actions to Kurtz's son, to become the **caretaker** of his memory.

The photographer opens his speech with the question 'Why? Huh? Why would a nice guy like you wanna kill the genius?', perhaps a reference to Conrad's Kurtz, one of a new breed, like Marlow, and a 'universal genius'. His observation that 'The man is clear in his mind, but his soul is mad' is taken from the eerie meeting between Marlow and Kurtz on the eve of their departure back down river from the Inner Station:

> 'Believe me or not, his intelligence was perfectly clear – concentrated, it is true, upon himself with horrible intensity, yet clear; and therein was my only chance – barring, of course, the killing of him there and then, which wasn't so good, on account of unavoidable noise. But his soul was mad.'

The photo-journalist says that 'He [Kurtz] reads poetry out loud and a voice. A voice.' The Russian trader tells Marlow, 'Ah! I'll never, never meet such a man again. You ought to have heard him recite poetry – his own too it was, he told me. Poetry!' However, it is Marlow who recalls the effect of hearing Kurtz: 'The volume of tone he emitted without effort, almost without the trouble of moving his lips, amazed me. A voice! a voice!'

This final section makes more and more sense the more often you see it, and this process of repeated viewing, existing somewhere in the realm between thorough research and obsession, leads to some odd conclusions – e.g. that not only is Dennis Hopper's role not bad and his dialogue meaningless waffle, but it is essential to the film as a whole. As much as any other ingredient it emphasises the film's chief literary source, and he seems perfectly cast. Still, Hopper makes an undeniably odd, druggy, comic turn as a man whose 'very existence was improbable, inexplicable, and altogether bewildering. He was an insoluble problem. It was inconceivable how he had existed, how he had succeeded in getting so far, how he had managed to remain – why he did not instantly disappear.'

Playboy Bunnies

In the United Services Overseas (USO) show sequence, just the set 'sure is a bizarre sight in the middle of this shit'. **Vietnam** Vet William Hokanson recalls that 'They did have these USO shows, but only in large, well-secured base camps, not on the edge of the **jungle**'. A bit of artistic licence, but, as a recent history of beauty pageants points out, 'Miss America winners and runners up were traditionally shipped off to Vietnam'.

Like so much else in the film, there was originally a great deal more of the Bunnies in the early cuts. Some of these ditched scenes are apparently to be found in the mythical **five-hour version**. After leaving **Hau Phat**, the **PBR** comes across **Bill Graham** and the three Bunnies with the **helicopter**, which has run out of fuel. **Willard** goes off for some recon and returns with a plan to exchange petrol for all his men to spend twenty minutes each with a Bunny. These encounters take place within abandoned helicopter fuselages. According to *Film Threat* magazine:

> **Chef**'s is an ex-bird performer and natters on about it while cradling a cockatoo. **Lance**'s Bunny [**Cindi Wood**] recounts the horrors of her Playmate of the Year photo shoot while **drug** fan **Lance** sucks oxygen from plastic tubes [Did this inspire **Dennis Hopper**'s inhalation of mysterious gas in *Blue Velvet*?], until she

accidentally topples a coffin and a dead body spills out, dousing the mood. Somewhere in the shuffle, **Clean** gets overlooked.

When asked if these sequences didn't make the final cut because they were simply underdeveloped, **John Milius** enigmatically responds, laughing, 'That had more implications, that was much more complicated than that. The real story must never be told.'

polio

Before asking **Willard** to become the **caretaker** of his memory **Kurtz** tells him the story that changed the way he saw the enemy, the way he saw the war:

> I remember when I was with Special Forces – it seems a thousand centuries ago – we went into a camp to inoculate the children. We'd left the camp after we had inoculated the children for polio and this old man came running after us and he was crying, and he couldn't see. We went back there and they had hacked off every inoculated arm and there they were in a pile, a pile of little arms and I remember I, I, I cried. I wept like some grandmother. I wanted to tear my teeth out. I didn't know what I wanted to do, and I want to remember it, I never want to forget it. I never want to forget, and then I realised like I was shot, like I was shot with a diamond, a diamond bullet went through my forehead and I thought, My God, the genius of that. The genius, the will to do that. Perfect, genuine, complete, crystalline, pure. And then I realised they were stronger than we, because they could stand it. These were not monsters, these were men, trained cadres. These men who fought with their hearts, who have families, who have children, who are filled with love. But they have the strength, the strength to do that. If I had ten divisions of these men then our troubles here would be over very quickly. You

have to have men who are moral and at the same time able to use their primordial instincts to kill without feeling, without passion, without judgement, without judgement. Because it's judgement that defeats us.

The notion of will is also of central importance to **Conrad**'s Kurtz. His report for the Society for the Suppression of Savage Customs includes the line 'By the simple exercise of our will we can exert a power for good practically unbounded'. As **John Milius** recalls, the incident with the hacked-off arms is based on fact:

> The story of the arms is really true. It happened to **Fred Rexer**, he told me the story. That was just one of the more unpleasant things that happened to him. Other than that, I think that Fred really enjoyed his war.

Pork Lips Now

This short film, directed by Ernie Fosselius, is an extended spoof of *Apocalypse Now*. It was shown at the 1980 Edinburgh Film Festival in tandem with *Werner Herzog Eats His Shoe*, directed by **Les Blank**, a cameraman on **Hearts of Darkness: A Filmmaker's Apocalypse**. It concerns a cook called Dullard on a mission that takes him across Los Angeles to Chinatown, where the renegade Mertz is undercutting local butchers. Its many allusions to *Apocalypse Now* include a man on roller skates being pulled behind a car.

puppy

See **sampan**.

pretentiousness

See **forty-seven different levels**.

'Purple Haze'

Jimi Hendrix was one of the sounds of **Vietnam**, according to **Michael Herr**, who first heard him while covering the war. It is his **music** that is playing on the GI's radio at **Do Long bridge**. In the cascade of iconic images in the demilitarised zone sequence before the firefight that kills **Clean**, **Lance** sets off a purple smoke canister and remarks approvingly, 'Purple Haze'. The oblique reference to Hendrix instantly calls to mind the image of a young black hero who would die before his time, so perhaps foreshadowing the fate of Clean and **Chief**. The song is one of the essential anthems of the 1960s, a codified **drug** song. Purple Haze was a type of LSD made by **acid** king Augustus Owsley Stanley III, 'the man who did for acid what Henry Ford did for the motor car'. It was made specially for Jimi Hendrix, who is said to have bought 100,000 doses.

Q

quadrophonic quintuphonic

Sound designer **Walter Murch** explains:

Francis [Coppola] had decided that he wanted quadrophonic sound on *Apocalypse Now*. Nobody really knew what that entailed. We knew what it meant technically, but nobody knew what it really meant in a theatrical setting. So that was one of my jobs – how to do this and in fact turn it into what has become the standard way of realising big motion picture sound. It is variously described as split-surrounded format, or 5.1 format. Instead of quadrophonic sound it's really quintuphonic in that there are five channels of full range information – three in the front and two in the back, and then one channel of low frequency enforcement only. This is the standard Dolby digital format and the DTS format. SDDS, the Sony format, has five channels of sound behind the screen, two channels in the back and then one low frequency.

The other thing was, how do you deal with this aesthetically? Nobody had ever done this before in a theatrical film. *Tommy* had done it a year or two earlier in a musical form, but to have it in a war film with scenes of dialogue and everything, how do you manipulate it?

One of the tasks I set myself was a chart of orchestration of how those channels would be used for sound effect and how they would be used for **music** and dialogue throughout the whole film. So there's a road map of where all those channels are engaged and where they aren't engaged. Because one of the principles that I dedicated myself to was not to have those channels on all at the same time. Because in the end it would either drive you crazy or you would become indifferent to it.

So the idea was to modulate the sound spacially so that for maybe ten minutes at a time the film collapses into a mono-phonic **soundtrack** – there is just sound coming out of the cen-tral speaker. Then for dramatic purposes it can open up to stereo, then open up even further to this quadrophonic/quintuphonic format. So you have layers of transition where you can open up and collapse back down. You can use those moments for dramatic purposes and the moments that are significant for sound effects are not necessarily significant for music.

It's quintuphonic at the beginning. The sound of the **heli-copter** goes from right back to left back, then to left front, then centre, then right front and then to the right back. We spread the echo of **The Doors** in the back. But the first real use of it is when they meet **Duvall** and you have that whole battle scene. From the first moment when they sight the helicopters until Duvall says, **'I love the smell of napalm'** – that's pretty much quintuphonic all the way. Then it collapses down to fairly modest stuff. But then, when they go into the **jungle**, looking for the mangoes, it opens up again into five channel sound, then it collapses. At the moment when they think they hear the **tiger** it all goes mono, so you're just looking at that place, then the tiger comes and it opens up when they start firing, and closes down again when he's on the boat thinking about **Kurtz**, looking at the dossier with the flashlight. Then when they arrive at **Hau Phat**, the **Playboy Bunnies** scene, it opens up into stereo, and when they move into the actual space of the auditorium, it opens up into quintuphonic and stays so throughout the whole concert and then collapses back down again.

Throughout the whole film it's alternating back and forth like that. I was thinking, What do I call what I've done? Because no one has ever done this before. What's the name for it? This has given me a three-dimensional space to decorate with sound. That's why a production designer has a title. You have an empty set that you decorate with visual stuff, I've sort of done the same thing with sound. He's called a production designer, I'll call myself a sound designer. The title had been used in the theatre before, but not really in film. It was a title whose time had come. The sound designer has been used to describe someone who comes up with the unusual sounds that aren't in any libraries, but that wasn't how I originated it. It wasn't that at all. It was somebody who was responsible for the architecture of the sound in a three-dimensional form.

R

racism

Chinua Achebe wrote an essay focusing on **Heart of Darkness** which aims to expose **Joseph Conrad** as a 'thoroughgoing racist'. This is contentious. How much did Conrad speak through his characters? Whatever, a sense of this unease exists in *Apocalypse Now*. It would be wrong to accuse the makers of *Apocalypse Now* of racism, but with its tone of moral ambiguity the film portrays an underlying racism in the **Vietnam War**. The French justified/defined their presence in South-east Asia as a *mission civilisatrice*, a concept at best condescending, at worst racist. The American involvement was in part at least an extension of this idea.

The film's most charismatic character, **Colonel Kilgore**, hates the **Viet Cong**, to some extent as an expedient for pursuing the conflict. He runs the full gamut of racist epithets, casually referring to the North Vietnamese enemy as **dinks**, **gooks** or **slopes**. This simply reflects the demonisation of the enemy, giving them jokey and insulting nicknames, and of war in general, and seems true to the way many soldiers spoke in **Vietnam**. Kilgore is not merely casually racist, though. One of his key lines that exposes his priorities is **'Charlie don't surf'**. This fact, which means that the point at the mouth of the **Nung river** that breaks both ways and has a fantastic peak is wasted, is the summation of his contempt for the North Vietnamese. It is this, almost as much as the sneaky bombing of a **Huey**, which makes him look down on them as 'fucking savages' and aspire, misquoting General Curtis E. LeMay, to 'blow them into the **Stone Age**'.

In the piece on racism in *Heart of Darkness* Achebe admits that in a story that is mediated through two narrators the point of view of the author himself is not so easily extrapolated, although the modern reader is made to feel uncomfortable with some of the language and attitudes. But, as in the frequently cited case of *Huckleberry Finn*, the word 'nigger' has changed dramatically in usage in the last hundred years. In *Apocalypse Now* critics have expressed a certain unease about a black commander always referred to as '**Chief**' being killed by a **spear**, as if the film-makers were presenting this as a racially, atavistically appropriate death. So here the audience is allowed to decide for itself what it thinks of Kilgore, of whom **Willard** says, 'He wasn't a bad officer, I suppose.'

Redford, Robert (b. 1937)

Born in Santa Monica, California. He became a major film star from the late 1960s onwards. Paramount was very keen for him or Ryan O'Neal to play Michael Corleone in *The Godfather*. **Coppola** resolutely and wisely insisted on **Pacino**. Redford starred in *The Great Gatsby*, scripted by Coppola. He was one of the many early possibilities for the role of **Willard**. This would have upset the balance of the film. While effective in certain types of role, Redford is an actor who relies on a limited repertoire of mannerisms – wry smile, winsome grin, raised eyebrow, etc. – which he uses in every film. The role demands not a star, but an impassive actor who reins in his emotions.

relocation

In the scene in which **Willard** first meets **Kilgore** villagers are herded into an amphibious landing craft and cows air-lifted in the process of 'relocation'. An American official and a Vietnamese interpreter inform the villagers over loudspeakers; 'We will not hurt you. We are here to help you. We are here to extend a welcome hand to those of you who want to return to the arms of the South Vietnamese Government. This is an area controlled by the **Viet Cong** and North Vietnamese.'

In his 1971 book *Vietnam Inc.* the photographer Philip Jones Griffiths talks of America's plan to:

> transplant the villagers into urban enclaves, which loosens them from their traditional values and makes the imposition of new ones easier. This policy, euphemistically called 'relocation,' is the one constant of American strategy in **Vietnam**. 'Relocation' consists of destroying the fabric of rural society, using every military means possible to uproot the people and lay waste their homes for the purpose of creating a captive mass of people with their spirits broken in the hope of facilitating easier penetration with the new ideology.

Rexer, Fred

Fred Rexer Jr, a friend of **John Milius**, was employed on the film, along with Richard Dioguardi, as a military adviser, specifically on Special Forces. As Peter Cowie writes in *Coppola*, during the looping of the film Rexer turned up and 'regaled the **sound** engineers with stories of how, as a CIA operative, he had executed **Viet Cong** chieftains by squeezing his fingers through their eye-sockets and literally ripping their skulls apart'. He told Milius how he had witnessed the real scene of the pile of amputated arms of **polio**-inoculated Vietnamese children, the apocalyptic episode in which **Kurtz** became aware of the pure, crystalline genius of the enemy.

Rheault, Robert

The chief modern inspiration for **Brando**'s **Kurtz**. In *Brando* Peter Manso asserts that '*Apocalypse Now* had originally been conceived by screenwriter **John Milius** in 1969 as both an adaptation of **Conrad**'s

Heart of Darkness and a pro-war testament to the career of Robert Rheault.' He goes on mistakenly to claim that he was the inspiration for the character of **Kilgore**. Rheault was a **Green Beret** officer who was court-martialled in 1969 for allegedly ordering the execution of a Vietnamese guide suspected of being a double agent. As in the case of the four executed agents in *Apocalypse Now*, the suspicions were almost certainly well founded. Stanley Karnow writes in *Vietnam – A History*: 'Colonel Robert Rheault and his special forces team were charged with the summary execution of a suspected **Vietcong** spy, the alleged murder being labelled in official jargon as "**termination with extreme prejudice**".' Although the charges were eventually dropped, this case marked the end of Rheault's military career.

John Milius recalls:

> I remember in 1969 when that story came out about Rheault, which was hidden later on by the revelations about My Lai. My Lai was not the big deal, because My Lais happen in every war, but what happened to Robert Rheault was really interesting. The idea was that US troops were out there committing their own foreign policy. Remember, from 1963 onward, there were never any clear military objectives in the entire involvement in **Vietnam**. So this guy is doing his job, I mean he's trying to win. Eventually he is incarcerated, he is brought down for trying to win.

see **sampan**.

Rhythm Devils, the

On 25 October 1978, invited by **Bill Graham** (the **Playboy Bunnies**' agent in *Apocalypse Now*) **Francis Coppola**, **Eleanor** and their son Gian-Carlo attended a Grateful Dead concert in California. Eleanor Coppola recalls in *Notes*:

> The music was amazing. It had physical impact . . . There was a long sequence where just two drummers played . . . .

Something about the evening reminded me about the evening inside the **Ifugao** priest's house [Where she was invited to witness and share in tribal rituals]. It felt like the same thing. The scale was different, but everyone being joined together by rhythms and images was the same, and instead of rice wine and betel nut there was beer and grass.

The drummers were Mickey Hart and Bill Kreutzmann, and almost instantly Francis Coppola sensed that they could supply an appropriate percussive sound to complement the more conventional synthesiser **soundtrack** that he and his father, **Carmine Coppola**, oversaw. So the Rhythm Devils were formed for this one project and were made up of the two Grateful Dead drummers joined by Airto Moreira, Michael Hinton, Jim Loveless, Greg Errico, Jordan Amarantha, Flora Purim and Phil Lesh. In the Coppola tradition of family employment, Gian-Carlo served the project as an instrument builder and associate producer. All the musicians brought their own collections of instruments to the sessions and these were enhanced by newly built instruments created by 'updating ancient designs with modern materials and some electronic processing'. They played along as the film was screened in the studio.

The brief from Coppola was 'to conjure music not only relevant to **Vietnam** in the 60s, but which also extended back to the first man at the origins of his existence. The essence of the film is the primal myth of the King being killed and his **assassin** taking his place as the new King.'

The sleeve notes record that:

To simulate the sound of **napalm** (which became a symbolic sound underpinning much of the film) we used 'The Beam', a long aluminium I-beam with twelve bass piano strings stretched along its length; the vibration of the strings is sensed by a very large magnetic pickup. The sound is amplified through Meyers speakers and sub-woofers, whose loudness can be varied with a foot-pedal allowing a controlled degree of acoustic feedback.

With track titles such as 'The Compound', 'Trenches', 'Street Gang', '**Lance**', '**Kurtz**' and 'Napalm For Breakfast', the haunting percussion of the Rhythm Devils accompanies much of the **boat**'s journey, notably on the approaches to **Hau Phat** and **Do Long** and at the beginning of the sacrificial ritual scene, before seguing into '**The End**'.

'Ride of the Valkyries, The'

Music first heard briefly hummed in background in excited reaction to **Kilgore**'s decision to embark on a raid to capture the point and drop the boat in the mouth of the **Nung river** 'like a baby'. 'This is the First of the Ninth. **Air Cav**, son. Air Mobile.' It is then played over loudspeakers to accompany the dawn raid on the **Viet Cong** village – 'It scares the hell out of the **slopes**.' It is from *Die Walküre*, by Richard Wagner, conducted by Sir Georg Solti, and performed by the Vienna Philharmonic Orchestra. The 'Ride of the Valkyries' opens Act III with the daughters of Wotan and Erda gathering on top of a rocky mountain amidst fast-moving clouds and lightning, flying through the air on horseback carrying dead warriors from the battlefield to Valhalla. **Walter Murch** says in *Projections 6*:

> That was present in the story right from the beginning of the script and it's not actually far from the truth of some of these situations. You may recall something called Operation Just Cause in Panama where they were trying to flush Noriega out of the Vatican Consulate and they played **rock 'n' roll** and they thought he would kind of run out of the consulate because he couldn't stand the music any more. The film came out before that happened so, in some weird way, reality might have been

influenced by the film. Certainly the film was influenced by things that happened like this, not only in **Vietnam** but in other wars as well. When you boil it right down, just the idea of having bugles and drums which goes way back to the Egyptians, Greeks and maybe beyond is a form of this – that somehow organised sound that is very rhythmic and strident has a terrifying effect on the opposition.

Colonel William Hokanson recalls, 'Loudspeakers were used to encourage VC to "rally" to the government side. But this was done with Vietnamese music and native speakers, not with Wagner.' This piece of music has always had strong martial associations. It is the Regimental March of the British Parachute Regiment, was chosen as the soundtrack to accompany the Arnhem documentary recreation *Theirs is the Glory* in 1945 and features on the soundtrack of the Alan Ladd film *The Red Beret*. The use of Wagner is instantly powerful and unsettling. He was Hitler's favourite composer and his music played over the loudspeakers in the Nazi extermination camps.

This raid is one of the film's signature sequences, weaving together many elements of drama and cinematic technique in a brilliantly orchestrated whole. From the beginning it shows the formation-flying of **Hueys** – one of the features of the **Vietnam War** shown in newsreel footage. It captures the fear and excitement of being in an attack **helicopter**, described in *Chickenhawk*, **Dispatches** and elsewhere. At any time you can get blown up, shot down, get your balls blown off, freeze with fear; but while **Chef** cowers, **Clean** shouts out 'Run, **Charlie**!' as if he is at a football match. When Kilgore asks **Lance** what he thinks he says it's 'really exciting', but Kilgore was asking about the surf. Kilgore awards a case of beer for a successful hit.

This sequence was in **John Milius**'s script from the first draft. He recalls not expecting it to make it to the screen, 'Because it was so broad'. The scene was covered with as many cameras as they could get hold of – hence the slow-motion **napalm** explosion in the film's

opening scene. It also shows the attack from both sides, cutting from the approaching helicopters to the village, where the sound of distant but approaching engines and music is already creating panic.

It is in this complex sequence of rapidly changing viewpoint, quick cuts and various **sound** sources – music, dialogue, weaponry, helicopter – that sound and picture **editing** become crucial. The photography is sensational, using new camera equipment and anamorphic lenses, especially the wide shot of the napalm exploding the line of trees, a perfect collision of violence and beauty. The pacing of the editing is clever, alternating between frenetic and more leisurely.

In the **sound design** and editing Walter Murch applied his 'rule of 2½' which he had developed on *THX 1138*: 'It has to do with how many conceptual layers of sound you can deal with it one time.' As he says in *Projections 6*:

I began to be sensitive to this strange twilight zone between the numbers two and three – that up until two you had to pay very specific attention to the elements out of which you were constructing something. When you got to three or more, it became almost immaterial how many elements you were composing the thing out of . . . .

So, in mixing, you are playing the mixing board the way you would play a piano so that there were only two dominant sounds happening at the same time – helicopters and music, maybe a little bit of voice, but that's it: no footsteps, no gunfire. Now, if you want to make the point of a little bit of gunfire, you have to get rid of something, get rid of maybe a little bit of that voice and add a bit of gunfire in its place, or get rid of all the music completely. For example, when the boy says, 'I'm not going, I'm not going,' there's no music at all. On a certain logical level that is not reasonable because he is actually in the helicopter that is producing the music, so if anything it should be louder than anywhere else. The problem is, if you played it at that level, you wouldn't get the benefit of either. You are watching the film and you are involved in the story dramatically. Your impression when the scene is over is that everything has been played at full volume all the time. In fact, that is not true.

On a pedantic level, when dropping off the soldiers the helicopters occasionally linger a little too long or seem to stop, while accounts of Huey pilots testify to the speed with which this would happen – get down, count to three, get out and usually everyone was out before the count of two. Also, in *Past Imperfect – History According to the Movies*, Frances Fitzgerald points out:

> **Coppola**'s recreation of a Vietcong village is fairly accurate, but there couldn't have been any flag-flying villages intact on the coast after 1965 because the Americans had complete control of the air and such a village would have been too easy a target.

This whole sequence also represents another example of the creative paring down, cutting away unnecessary excess material, that was so essential to the film's ultimate genius. In early cuts it continued, with Lance stealing Kilgore's surf board. As it is, it ends perfectly with Kilgore's wistful observation **'Some day this war's gonna end'**.

rock 'n' roll war

The **Vietnam War** was the first TV war, but also the first rock 'n' roll war. The way **Michael Herr** captures the feeling of **Vietnam** in *Dispatches*, rock stars were heroic figures to the young fighters; they would carry around pictures of **Jimi Hendrix** and the Beatles as often as pictures of Martin Luther King and **Kennedy**. The music was so ubiquitous that it provided a **soundtrack** to the whole experience.

Rolling Stones, the

See **'(I Can't Get No) Satisfaction'**.

Roos, Fred (b. 1934)

Co-producer born in Santa Monica. Much of his early career was as a casting director; he worked on *Five Easy Pieces* (he also worked as producer on *Back Door to Hell* and *Flight to Fury* starring **Nicholson**, and as associate producer on *Drive, He Said*, which he directed), *The Godfather* and *American Graffiti* before working as a co-producer on *The Conversation*. He has gone on to work as producer, co-producer or executive producer on all **Coppola**'s films, as well as others from the Coppola stable such as *Hammett* and **Hearts of Darkness: A Filmmaker's Apocalypse**.

Ryan, Doug

A captain in the US Marines, Ryan worked on the film as an adviser on special unit military tactics.

S

sacrifice

The discovery of the **Ifugao** ritual sacrifice of a cow was a fortuitous one, allowing the dramatic cross-cutting between its violent death and the fleetingly depicted assassination of **Kurtz**. The close connection between these two deaths reinforces the theme of **the Fisher King** myth, suggested by several volumes in **Kurtz's library**, which in most of its variations is a fertility myth – a tale of regeneration connecting the notions of the assassin becoming king and the land once more becoming fertile. This sequence always retains its ability to shock with the reality of its violence, the swinging of the long-handled machetes wielded by **Willard** and the sacrificers. Eagle-eyed viewers will have noticed that the film does not end with the notice that 'No animals were harmed in the production of this motion picture'.

Saigon

Capital of South **Vietnam** and starting point of the story. After the final withdrawal of all American forces the North Vietnamese crushed the South Vietnamese army in 1975, the United States closed its embassy, Vietnam was reunified and Saigon was renamed **Ho Chi Minh** City.

'Saigon. Shit!'

The great first line. It is an immediate introduction to the film's counter-intuitive logic. **Willard** is upset that he is 'still only in

Saigon', not because he is not back home, but because he is not back in the **jungle**.

See **beginning, the**.

sampan

In *Hearts of Darkness: A Filmmaker's Apocalypse* **Albert Hall** says that **Coppola** encouraged his actors to improvise as much as possible and that this sequence was based on their improvisation. But the scene was in fact written (apart from the last line, which was supplied by **John Milius**) by **Walter Murch** and Coppola in the shooting break in the summer of 1976 while the sets were being rebuilt after having been destroyed by a typhoon. The idea was to show the boat and the crew carrying out one of their jobs, acting as 'a police boat – to stop suspicious boats. . . . The specific idea of the scene was to present a kind of mini My Lai massacre.'

The device of having these ordinary Vietnamese river traders mown down because the **woman** is reaching out to protect her puppy is not the film's subtlest moment. But it effectively presents a 'slaughter of the innocents' episode, of which My Lai is perhaps the most resonant example from the **Vietnam War**. In March 1968 an American infantry platoon acting under orders from its commanding officer Lieutenant William Calley Jr slaughtered 347 Vietnamese inhabitants of this small coastal village in cold blood.

The preparation of this scene marks a perfect example of the schism, the creative balance, that existed between John Milius, the war-lover, and Francis Coppola, the liberal exploring his guilt. Milius says:

> I never liked the scene where they stopped the boat. I said this shouldn't be in the movie. It's typical, you've got to have a My Lai, you've got to run down the American soldier. Francis said,

'The audience has come to really like these guys. The audience is on the boat with these guys. The important thing now is to make the audience share in the guilt. So, in the end, I really liked the scene. But of course the end of the scene is really typical of me, where **Chief** says that they have to take the wounded woman to a friendly hospital, and **Willard** shoots her and says, 'I told you not to stop.'

A specialist mistake-spotter has criticised an element of this sequence which comes to light after they have gunned down the Vietnamese family:

The comic relief is the immediate close-up of Mr **Clean**, leaning over his weapon, wide-eyed – surely surprised because the belted .308 feeding into his M.60 consists of BLANKS (obvious from their recessed red tips).

This may be true, but it isn't so surprising, surely. Still, it would certainly have lent the production an extra layer of realism and irony to spray the family with real bullets, especially as they were portrayed by South Vietnamese boat people who had fled the country two weeks before the sampan scene was shot.

saucier

See **Chef**.

Sheen, Martin (b. 1940)

My hair was on fire and I was trying to put it out with a hammer.
                                                                Martin Sheen

Born Ramon Estevez in Dayton, Ohio. He won a trip to New York as a prize in an acting competition. Having changed his name in 1960, he spent the next decade making his name as an actor, mostly on television. After a small role in *Catch-22*, he broke through with his brilliant performance as a charismatic sociopath in *Badlands*. He had already been considered to play Michael Corleone in *The Godfather*, but it is surely his ability to play the quiet, intense, ruthless killer Charles Starkweather that recommended him for the role of **Willard**. It is his studied stillness that creates a calm at the centre of a crazed, pacy film; he is in virtually every shot and it is through his eyes and from his perspective that we see the action.

His experiences on the film were famously gruelling. In May 1976, when the production was hit by Typhoon Olga, Sheen went home with his family to Malibu. He realised that he simply didn't want to return to the film and tried unsuccessfully to negotiate a pay increase: '**Francis [Coppola]** had to really wrangle with me and negotiate to get me to do anything. I didn't trust anybody.'

He used the break to allay one of his practical fears: 'I couldn't swim and, look, we were spending all that time on the boat. I was very concerned about that. After this terrible storm came and ended shooting for a while, we came back for a few weeks to regroup and I took swimming lessons.'

The intensity of the role, the rigours of the shoot, Sheen's already fragile mental state, exacerbated by bad diet, heavy smoking and drinking, all mounted up and eventually he suffered a nervous collapse and near-fatal **heart attack** on 5 March 1977. Although he quickly regained physical health and returned within six weeks to complete his heroic contribution to the film, he was profoundly affected by the episode as he related in *Martin Sheen: Actor and Activist*:

> My near-death experience made me frightened and I realised that I was lacking and I wanted to get back to the church. And I did go back, but for a very short time, because I was really coming out of my fear. I was afraid that God would smite me

for my sins. That lasted for a very short time, and so I continued on my journey for another four years.

His use of the expression 'for my sins' is interesting (although not surprising from a devout Catholic). It echoes Willard's line from the beginning of the film: 'I wanted a mission, and for my sins, that's what I got.' This in turn quotes **Heart of Darkness**, when **Marlow** talks of **Kurtz**'s soul being mad after having looked in on itself: 'I had – for my sins, I suppose – to go through the ordeal of looking into it myself.'

Sheen got so bad that more than once he wandered down city streets, stopping strangers to ask them if they believed in God. He concluded: 'If you wanted to know what it was like or who I was at that time, it's on the screen. I was that person. I was a terribly unhappy man, going through a lot of horrible things.'

shrimp

The General says to **Willard** as they sit down to lunch, 'I don't know how you feel about the shrimp, but if you try some you won't have to prove your courage in any other way.' Willard silently refuses and, tellingly, it is only the dangerous, taciturn civilian who eats some.

slopes

Kilgore explains to **Lance** that he plays Wagner on his **helicopter** raids because 'it scares the shit out of the slopes'. The insulting term 'slopie' was used from World War II onwards by American, British and Australian servicemen. It had some general application for East Asians, but usually referred to Chinese.

snail

See **Kurtz**.

'Some day this war's gonna end'

See **'I love the smell of napalm in the morning'**; 'Ride of the Valkyries, The'.

sound/sound design

See **Murch, Walter**; **quadrophonic/quintuphonic**.

soundtrack

The soundtrack music to the film consists of:

- a synthesiser score, written by **Francis** and **Carmine Coppola**, performed by Patrick Gleeson, Richard Beggs, Bernard L. Krause, Don Preston, Shirley Walker and Nyle Steiner;
- a percussion score written and performed by **the Rhythm Devils**;
- **'The End'**, at **the beginning** and **end**;
- **'(I Can't Get No) Satisfaction'**, by the Rolling Stones – on Forces Radio, accompanying **Lance**'s **water-skiing**;
- **'The Ride of the Valkyries'** from **Die Walküre**, by Richard Wagner, performed by the Vienna Philharmonic Orchestra and conducted by Sir Georg Solti – accompanies the **Air Cavalry**'s dawn raid;
- 'Let the Good Times Roll', by Leonard Lee – sung by **Clean** while driving the boat, on the night after the **tiger** incident;
- **'Suzie Q'** by Flash Cadillac, over the **Playboy Bunnies** show;
- 'Love Me, And Let Me Love You', the song that **Robert Duvall** sings, heard faintly in the background during the camp-fire scene;

- 'Mnong Gar Music from **Vietnam**' – credited but inaudible in the release version of the film.

spear

After the attack of tiny **arrows** – taken directly from *Heart of Darkness* – and ignoring the advice of **Willard**, the **Chief** shouts at him furiously: 'You got us into this mess and now you can't get us out, because you don't know where the hell you're going, do you? Do you?!' He takes a machine-gun and starts firing indiscriminately at the **Montagnards** on the river bank. Standing outside the cabin he receives a spear (presumably meant for Willard) through the heart. As the unhelmed boat spins slowly, he utters his final disbelieving words, 'A spear', and falls elegantly with a half-turn, to be caught by Willard.

In *Heart of Darkness* **Marlow** likewise shouts at the helmsman to 'Steer her straight', but he ignores him and joins the pilgrims, 'simply squirting lead into that bush'. In the confusion and smoke:

'We tore away slowly along the overhanging bushes in a whirl of broken twigs and flying leaves ... I threw my head back to a glinting whizz that traversed the pilot-house, in at one shutterhole and out at the other. Looking past that mad helmsman, who was shaking the empty rifle and yelling at the shore, I saw vague forms of men running bent double, leaping, gliding, indistinct, incomplete, evanescent. Something big appeared in the air before the shutter, the rifle went overboard, and the man stepped back swiftly, looked at me over his shoulder in an extraordinary, profound, familiar manner, and fell upon my feet. The side of his head hit the wheel twice, and the end of what appeared to be a long cane clattered round and

knocked over a little camp-stool. It looked as though after
wrenching that thing from somebody ashore he had lost his
balance in the effort. The thin smoke had blown away, we
were clear of the snag, and looking ahead I could see that
in another hundred yards or so I would be free to sheer
off, away from the bank; but my feet felt so very warm
and wet that I had to look down. The man had rolled
on his back and stared straight up at me; both his hands
clutched that cane. It was the shaft of a spear that, either
thrown or lunged through the opening, had caught him in
the side just below the ribs; the blade had gone in out of
sight, after making a frightful gash; my shoes were full; a
pool of blood lay very still, gleaming dark-red under the
wheel; his eyes shone with an amazing lustre. The fusillade
burst out again. He looked at me anxiously, gripping the
spear like something precious, with an air of being afraid I
would try to take it away from him . . . he died without
uttering a sound, without moving a limb, without twitching
a muscle.'

In *Apocalypse Now*, as Willard cradles him, in a moment of perverse
horror Chief grabs Willard and expends his last energy trying to pull
his face on to the spear. Willard forces his head back and Chief at
last dies. This dark punch-line serves as a modern rendition of the
uncomfortable, hypocritical relationship between Marlow and the
helmsman. **Conrad**'s own view is implicit in the absurd reaction
to the helmsman's sticky end. Marlow is at first concerned for his
shoes and the probability of **Kurtz**'s own death before thinking
of the helmsman. **The Company**, through him, is responsible for
the dangerous mission, just as the CIA and Willard are ultimately
responsible for the deaths of three-quarters of the boat's crew, and
the Chief knows it.

Spradlin, G. D. (b. 1920)

The actor who plays **the General** in the **Nha Trang** lunch/mission sequence. Born in Daylight Township, Oklahoma. Among his film appearances are an uncredited role in *Tora! Tora! Tora!*, the TV movie *Robert Kennedy and His Times* (as **Lyndon Johnson**), *The War of the Roses* and Reverend Lemon in *Ed Wood*. His most notable role prior to *Apocalypse Now* was as the deeply nasty Senator Geary in *The Godfather Part II*.

Star Wars

The project that **George Lucas** moved on to when it became apparent that he wouldn't direct *Apocalypse Now*. **Walter Murch** explains:

> So he sat down and had a long think: 'What was it about **Vietnam** that I really wanted to explore in *Apocalypse Now*? What was the core story?' It was the story of a small tribe of people who were somehow able, through their spirit, to withstand the assault of the Empire, the mightiest military force in the galaxy at that time. And so he took that story that he wanted to tell and transposed it out of any political and social context, and set it in a galaxy far, far away. He managed to make it on his own terms without any direct allusions to what he was really doing. The rebels are in fact the Vietnamese, the Empire is in fact the US Army. So *Star Wars* was really George's way of making *Apocalypse Now*.

John Milius comments: 'George likes to take credit for things, saying that he thought up the idea of *Apocalypse Now*, but all you have to do is see that movie, his version of Vietnam, and you know that it's not true.'

Sternberg, Tom

Co-producer. This marked his first collaboration with **Coppola**.

Stockton, Colonel John B.

One of the real-life inspirations for the character of **Kilgore**.

Stone Age

When **Kilgore** calls a **napalm** strike on the forest to secure the beach for **surfing**, his final order is to 'Blow them into the Stone Age, son'. This is a reference to the famous statement made by General Curtis E. LeMay, the Head of US Strategic Air Command, and the model for the George C. Scott character, General Buck Turgidson, in *Dr Strangelove*. In 1965 he said, 'My solution to the problem would be to tell them [the North Vietnamese] frankly that they have got to draw in their horns and stop their aggression, or we're going to bomb them back into the Stone Age.'

Storaro, Vittorio (b. 1940)

Director of photography, born in Rome. He asserts that 'the visual composition of the frame and the camera movement within a shot are simply the words and sentences of a paragraph. The director is responsible for the paragraph and the cinematographer's contributions make up the sentences within it.' He has forged significant partnerships with three film directors: Bernardo Bertolucci (*The Conformist, Last Tango in Paris, 1900, The Last Emperor*, etc.); Warren Beatty (*Reds, Ishtar*, produced by and starring Beatty, and *Dick Tracy*); and **Coppola** (*Apocalypse Now, One From the Heart, Tucker: The Man and His Dream, New York Stories*). He won **Academy Awards** for *Apocalypse Now, Reds* and *The Last Emperor*.

Interviewed in *Projections 6*, he talks of how:

The original idea was to depict the impact of one culture which had been superimposed over another culture . . . The Americans, as depicted in the film, were out of place; where people live and think in a different way, a more primitive way. They were bringing their culture with them, which was also their mentality, so they didn't understand the people they were at war with. If they understood this culture, they would have thought differently about the war fought in this land. This was the tragedy of the story, really.

This contrast between the two cultures, the notion of contrast, is the central idea behind Storaro's cinematography in the film:

Often, we tried to use colour and light to create the mood of conflict in subtle ways. The way that a red fire in a camp contrasted to the blue or black gun in the foreground, or the way the colour of a **weapon** stood out against the sunset, or how an American soldier with a blackened face was seen against the green **jungle** or blue sky. All of that helped to create the mood and tell the story. Even the **surfing** sequence indicated a collision of energies, that something was askew, out of context, unnatural to that environment.

This notion of contrast naturally reaches its height at the climax of the journey with the appearance of **Kurtz**, the representative of 'the dark side of civilisation . . . When I pictured these scenes before we shot them, I always saw **Brando** in the shadows or partially lit.'

The greatness of the film is the result of all the ingredients working together, and the cinematography is of course central to this success. Watching the film with no sound you are reminded that the camera work is immaculate, every shot perfectly lit and perfectly framed. Scene by scene, the whole look of the film is deliberately, beautifully constructed. This sumptuous visual quality is one of the chief reasons for the film retaining its power to dazzle and shock, and also a key factor in creating the ambiguous, uncomfortable feel. From the opening sequence with the arresting slow-motion **napalm** explosion we are confronted with the beauty of conflict shown alongside the pain and death of it. Thanks in large part to Storaro, war has never looked so good.

The superior definition evident in this film is partly down to the use of new anamorphic lenses produced by the Italian Technovision company. The main camera used was the Cinema Products' X35R. According to Barry Salt's *Film Style & Technology*, the new model:

> was in fact just a refined version of the Mitchell camera, designed with an integral mirror reflex shutter, and weighing 93 Ibs. without lens and film. It had a single lens mount of the BNCR pattern, which meant that all those old Mitchell lenses could be still used, and its noise level was just suitable for studio use. The improvements made to the design by Cinema Products included a shutter which stopped closed, and a new stroke length and entry adjustment for the claw.

For Storaro, as for everyone involved in the project:

> It was very difficult work. Very, very difficult. *Apocalypse Now* was the sum of my work up to that time. . . . It was through **Conrad**, in part, and the title of his novella **Heart of Darkness** on which Coppola's film is based, that I began to re-evaluate everything that went before. The concept of 'darkness' was revealing. It is where light ends. But I also realised that darkness is not the absence of light but the antithesis of light. In other words, they are aspects of each other. Light and dark are not only metaphors but the means by which we perceive and understand.

Storaro plays the newsreel cameraman, alongside Coppola's director, in the scene when the crew of the **PBR** first meet the **Air Cavalry**.

surfing

Surfing is one of the film's key images, representing the illogic, the madness of America's involvement in **Vietnam**. But it is also simply surfing. The beaches of central Vietnam are very good for surfing, though not so much those at the mouth of the **Mekong river**, which presumably should be seen as the point where the **Air Cavalry** makes its dawn raid, described by **Kilgore**'s junior officer as a 'fantastic peak' and 'tube city'.

There have been several surf movies, but not enough to constitute a separate genre. *Crystal Voyager* is a perfect celluloid encapsulation of the stoned early 1970s, pretty but phenomenally tedious, almost totally bogus, apart from the bitching final sequence accompanied by Pink Floyd's 'Echoes'. *Blue Juice* and *Point Break* are similarly flawed, silly but fun, very nearly tubular. The two surf movies that touch greatness – **Big Wednesday** and *Apocalypse Now* – have Vietnam and **John Milius** in common. They're both totally rad. Milius says of the surfing scenes:

> I just saw it as being outrageous. It was the sort of thing that was happening out there. I look on Vietnam as a Californian War. The Californian culture impacted itself on this ancient Asian way of life. Everything was Californian. People were putting flame jobs on **helicopters**, naming tanks after **rock 'n' roll** songs, airplanes having slogans, paisley painted bombs, putting different guns on the helicopter, stealing things so that your **Huey** could have more power, more guns, more potential than the next. The same thing with the way uniforms were worn. The idea was to present the powerful economic force behind the American war effort.

Surfing is part of that. Surfing was a big part of my life for a long time. Surfing is a mystical thing, but is also this useless Californian thing – it doesn't achieve anything, it is a frivolity. But at the same time it is kind of grand. I remember I came up with the idea for the surfing sequence when I was reading about the Six Day War. I think it was Ariel Sharon who went all the way down to Aqaba, he took Aqaba, and then he went skin-diving. He got off the tank and he went skin-diving, and he speared some of these fish because they belonged to the Arabs. He could go home and say, 'I have their fish.' That's the same thing, 'We're gonna surf **Charlie**'s waves. We're gonna take everything from Charlie and surf his waves.'

'Suzie Q'

The song by Flash Cadillac that accompanies the **Playboy Bunnies** United Services Overseas show. It was written by Dale Hawkins and came to prominence when covered by Creedence Clearwater Revival as their first single in September 1968. It reached number 11 in the US charts, but failed to chart in Britain.

T

Tavoularis, Dean (b. 1932)

Production designer born in Lowell, Massachusetts. He worked on *Bonnie and Clyde*, *Candy*, *Zabriskie Point* and *Little Big Man* before his first job with **Coppola** on *The Godfather*. This collaboration has endured to the present. He won an **Oscar** for *The Godfather Part II* and was nominated for *The Brink's Job*, *Apocalypse Now*, *Tucker: The Man and His Dream* and *The Godfather Part III*. Of his contribution to *Apocalypse Now*, he said in the film's press release:

> The **Kurtz** compound took eight months to build using up to 600 labourers a day, working in the 2,000 year old techniques which the Khmer aborigines used – no power equipment at all, **carabao** and people pulling these 300-pound blocks which totalled thousands, thousands . . . nobody had built anything like it. The B-52 tail – we got the dimensions from a Mattel model, the way the Russians do – it was about 80 feet tall. They built it piece by piece in a little fabrication shop in Manila and then they brought it out to the set and put it together and it worked.

The typhoon was a major occurrence for Tavoularis. As he recalls in Peter Cowie's *Coppola*:

> The typhoon eventually passed, and we went round surveying the damage. Everything was covered in mud. The insurance people arrived from Hong Kong and worked out this arrangement whereby we would stop working for several months,

reorganise everything at a single location, and then try to do the remainder of the film. We rebuilt down south, and in some degree when you have the chance to rebuild a set, it's a gift.

Producer **Gray Frederickson** has recalled in *Film Threat* some macabre set decorations instigated by Tavoularis:

I remember the production designer [Dean Tavoularis] joking around that they were going to get some real bodies in there, and I didn't believe them; I didn't think it would happen. I went to the set one day, and the prop man said, 'Come over here, let me show you something.' And I went back in a little tent behind the mess tent, and there were a bunch of bodies on the ground, covered with tarpaulins. And they were preserved in formaldehyde or something. I said, 'You can't do that! We can't have that, it's crazy! I mean, you can't have real dead bodies. Where did they come from?' And he said, 'Oh, well, we found a guy who supplies them to the local medical schools and they use them for cadavers.' Word went around and around for a while, and then all of a sudden it got to the military and they checked on the guy who got them, and it turned out that he didn't supply them. He was just some guy who robbed graves and brought them there. So then they came back and started an investigation. They took our passports away from us. They said, 'How do we know you didn't kill these people?'

See **temple**; **Wood, Cyndi**.

temple

Kurtz's temple compound was, as **Dean Tavoularis** explained, a remarkable enterprise, and its construction ran parallel with one of the central themes of the film as discussed by **Vittorio Storaro**. It was a complex design and engineering feat using ancient methods in the midst of a hugely expensive modern, Western production of a film that explores the idea of the ancient and modern clashing, and the superimposition of one culture on another.

The complex is closely based on the ruined, overgrown Cambodian temple of **Angkor Wat**. Like its inspiration in Cambodia and Kurtz's Inner Station, the temple compound seems to spring from the **jungle**, which is all the time threatening to swallow it up. The Buddha sculptures seen at **the beginning** and **end** of the film provide a link back to **Conrad**. In the final paragraph of *Heart of Darkness*, when **Marlow** has finished his story, the unnamed narrator takes over once again to conclude the book, and begins: 'Marlow ceased and sat apart, indistinct and silent, in the pose of a meditating Buddha.' The sculptures look like copies of carvings from Angkor Wat. The film has quite unfairly been criticised in this aspect. It is said that if, as is likely, the **Nung river** is supposed to be seen as the **Mekong**, then how could the **boat** end up at Angkor Wat, which is in north-west Cambodia, when travelling up the Mekong would lead them towards Phnom Penh, then north-east and north into Laos. But despite the similarity, the compound shouldn't be seen to stand for Angkor Wat.

It was while watching the construction of the temple complex for the film that **Eleanor Coppola** had her own apocalypse, mentioned in *Notes*.

See **Zoetrope**.

'terminate with extreme prejudice'

One of the film's most famous lines, spoken by the civilian in **Nha Trang**. The tone and impact of the line have, I think, a loose parallel in **Conrad**. At the Inner Station, **Marlow** and the Manager discuss **Kurtz**:

'"Nevertheless, I think Mr Kurtz is a remarkable man," I said with

emphasis. He started, dropped on me a cold heavy glance, said
very quietly, "He *was*," and turned his back on me.'

Both statements instantly consign Kurtz to the past tense. Regarding
the expression itself, 'terminate with extreme prejudice' appeared in
news accounts from the time of the war. According to Colonel
William Hokanson:

> 'Terminate' is a euphemism for firing someone. 'Extreme preju-
> dice' meant execute. It had no racial connotation, but was a play
> on the expression used in the personnel field. When someone
> had not worked out in a position through no fault of his own,
> he would be transferred or reassigned 'without prejudice' (to
> his future career). Needless to say, 'extreme prejudice' ended
> your career.

terror

While it is suggested that **Conrad**'s **Kurtz** only confronts the horror
right at the end, **Brando**'s Kurtz has prepared himself for the moment
and made friends of horror and moral terror. Otherwise they are
enemies to be feared. The film just about gets away with this,
especially as it is beautifully filmed, but it has the feel of a preparatory
improvisation, to get Brando into character, to muse on the notion
of horror, which will be the last thing on Kurtz's mind.

tiger

The tiger was as real, close and scary as it looks, according to **Frederic
Forrest** in *Hearts of Darkness: A Filmmaker's Apocalypse*:

> That was really crazy, that time with me and Marty [**Sheen**]
> and the tiger. Yeah, that was just insane. We had this guy with
> the tiger, a couple, the trainers and he had a (adopts speech

impediment) slight speech impediment, and had scar tissue all over his face where he had these fights with the tiger, Gamby.

The trainer used a pig on a string as a bait to get the tiger to do what they wanted and he would arrive on set and say:

'Gamby's very hungry today, **Martin** he's very hungry, Mr **Coppola**. I'm sure he will do exactly what you want. I haven't fed him in a week.' Oh shit! . . . I've never been so frightened in my life. To me, that was the essence of the whole film and **Vietnam** – the look in that tiger's eyes. The madness, like it didn't matter what you wanted, there was no reality any more. If that tiger wanted you, you were his.

Toledo

A city in north Ohio, the birthplace of **Willard**. **Kurtz** asks him how far he is from the **Ohio river**. He tells him about 200 miles, which is coincidentally the approximate distance between Toledo and **Martin Sheen**'s birthplace of Dayton, Ohio.

U

United Artists

The production company which initially invested $7.5 million in the project to secure US distribution rights. Steven Bach writes in *Final Cut* of how nervous the studio was becoming, during the lengthy post-production, that the film 'was not technically a United Artists (UA) production':

> To have closed **Coppola** down would have been an automatic write-off of the $30 million or so already expended [although a chunk of this had been covered personally by Coppola]. If the picture failed, UA would be in the uncomfortable position of enforcing the provisions of its loans to Coppola, attaching the assets not only of **Zoetrope** but of the man himself.

The possibility of evicting Coppola and his family from their Pacific Heights home was taken quite seriously.

But Bach and UA needn't have worried about *Apocalypse Now*. It became an artistic triumph, and a decent commercial success for the studio. It was Coppola's fellow Italian-American Michael Cimino (who had beaten him to the punch with *The Deer Hunter*) who would bring United Artists to its knees with *Heaven's Gate*.

V

Viet Cong

In 1941, when Japan invaded French Indo-China, **Ho Chi Minh** returned in secret to his native country for the first time in thirty years. Meeting up with sympathisers, he established a communist nationalist movement, the Viet Nam Doc Lap Dong Minh, the League for an Independent **Vietnam**, soon shortened to the Vietminh. It was this group and its army that defeated the French in the 1946–54 war. In 1960 Diem, the American-sanctioned leader of South Vietnam gave the Vietminh the pejorative nickname Viet Nam Cong San, the Vietnamese communists, which was immediately shortened to Viet Cong. The name stuck, hence VC and **Charlie**, derived from the radio call sign Victor Charlie.

Vietnam

Vietnam contains fifty-four ethnic groups, although 90 per cent of its population is Viet. Because of its strategically important geographical position and its natural resources – tin and rubber in the north, agriculture in the south – Vietnam has spent most of its history repelling aggression or seeking independence. In 1887, after continual incursions into Vietnam by its neighbour China, the French, having been involved in Vietnam since the early seventeenth century, colonised a sizeable part of the South-east Asian peninsula, creating the Indo-Chinese Union. It constituted Cochin-China, Tonkin and Amman (which make up modern Vietnam), Cambodia and Laos. From

1941–5 the area was overseen by French administrators under Japanese control. After the war the French attempted to resume control, were resisted by the Vietminh and, after a short-lived peace accord, the Indo-Chinese war began in December 1946.

In 1949 France recognised the independence of both Laos and Cambodia, but the war continued with ever-increasing American material support. France's catastrophic defeat at Dien Bien Phu in May 1954 marked the end of the war and the end of French control in South-east Asia.

Vietnam War

In *Vietnam: A History* Stanley Karnow writes that, 'In human terms at least, the war in **Vietnam** was a war that nobody won – a struggle between victims.' Looked at with hindsight, much of it seems senseless. In his review of Lieutenant-General Philip B. Davidson's *Vietnam At War* in *The Times* in January 1989, William Jackson asks the big question: 'Why did the Americans win all the major battles in Vietnam and yet lose the war?' It was a virtual continuation of the Indo-Chinese war of 1946–54. It had no proper beginning. Its official start, marked by the Gulf of Tonkin resolution passed by the US Congress on 7 August 1964, came as the result of reported but disputed North Vietnamese attacks on the *USS Maddox* and *Turner Joy*. But in fact the war can be traced back at least as far as 1959, when the North Vietnamese launched an attack near Bien Hoa, in which two American advisers were killed.

The Geneva Conference of 1954 divided Vietnam into North and South at the seventeenth parallel and established a demilitarised zone around it. In the Cold War atmosphere America feared that the domino effect of the spread of communism in Eastern Europe might be repeated in Asia. If Vietnam, Laos and Cambodia followed China and Korea, what would be next? Towards the end of the Indo-Chinese war the American Government was providing up to 80 per cent of

France's military supplies. With the division of Vietnam, America gave military and financial support to a succession of ineffectual leaders. All the time the USA committed increasing numbers of troops to the country.

In 1960 there were 900 US 'advisers' in the country, in 1961 3,000 'personnel'. By the end of 1962 there were 11,000 troops; in 1963 **Kennedy** was assassinated and succeeded by **Lyndon Johnson**. The total number of US forces increased year by year: 1964 – 23,000; 1965 – 181,000; 1966 – 385,000; reaching its peak of 541,500 in the year of *Apocalypse Now*'s supposed setting, 1969, the year of **Ho Chi Minh**'s death. The previous year **Richard Nixon** had been elected president and promised to reduce gradually the American military presence. This withdrawal began in June 1969. The last ground troops left in August 1972, the last military personnel in March 1973. Nixon resigned in August 1974, in March 1975 the **Viet Cong** captured the central highlands, on 29 April VC troops entered **Saigon** and the following day President Van Minh announced an unconditional surrender.

The American presence was justified by the US fear of communism, which led to incursions into Laos and Cambodia during Nixon's presidency. But their policy once there was either inchoate or senseless. As Jonathan Schell writes in *The Real War*:

It is a key fact about American policy in Vietnam that the withdrawal of American troops was built into it from the start. None of the presidents who waged war in Vietnam contemplated an open-ended campaign; all promised the public that American troops would be able to leave in the not-too-remote future. The promise of withdrawal precluded a policy of occupation of the colonial sort, in which a great power imposes its will on a small one indefinitely . . . and it dictated the need, as a matter not so much of idealism as of basic strategy, to build a regime in South Vietnam that could survive American departure . . . American

policy in Vietnam was called imperialistic. But it is a strange sort
of imperialism that foresees departing its colonial possession even
before it has seized it.

The Americans tried and failed to mould a sustainable anti-communist
political and military structure in Vietnam. Meanwhile, the tactic
employed to break the North Vietnamese was to begin in 1965, a
policy of relentless aerial assault with 'Operation Rolling Thunder'. In
1969, at the height of the war, the US Air Force made approximately
200,000 sorties. It dropped more bombs on North Vietnam than were
dropped in the whole of World War II. Neil Sheehan writes in *A Bright
Shining Lie*:

> By the end of 1966, fighter-bomber sorties were up to 400 a
> day. Each day, if one included the B-52s, about 825 tons of
> bombs and other explosives and other air munitions were let
> loose on a country the size of the state of Washington [just
> over 60,000 square miles]. From the window of an airplane or
> the open door of a **helicopter** the big brown blotches of the
> bomb craters disfigured the beauty of the Vietnamese landscape
> in every direction.

More stark statistics of the military punishment of the war are given
by Nguyen Khac Vien in his essay '*Apocalypse Now* Viewed by a
Vietnamese':

> Abstract figures which so far have only met with indifference
> now take on concrete shapes and come to life: 7,093 million
> tons of bombs dropped by planes, 7,016 million tons by ground
> **weapons**, 156 million tons by the navy, altogether 14,205
> million tons of lethal devices, 72,354 million litres of defoliants,
> some of which may cause cancer or deformed babies; 577
> kilograms of ammunition per head of population.

Fifty-six thousand Americans died in the Vietnam War. The number of Vietnamese, North and South, who died can only be estimated, but in 1969 General Vo Nguyen Giap, the North Vietnamese military commander, admitted to a journalist that they had lost over 500,000. In 1968 they lost 37,000 in the Tet Offensive alone. It was in the attitude to casualties in the coverage of the war that America's defeat became inevitable. The American people, unsure of the reasons and justifications for their country's involvement in South-east Asia to begin with, were daily confronted on TV by images of death and violence. The North Vietnamese had no media problems – almost no media – and were engaged in a civil war, a war for independence and self-determination. As Stanley Karnow records:

> 'Every minute, hundreds of thousands of people die on this earth,' General Giap once said, and [like Ho Chi Minh] he discounted 'the life or death of a hundred, a thousand, tens of thousands of human beings, even our compatriots.' During the war against the Americans, he spoke of fighting ten, fifteen, twenty, fifty years, regardless of cost, until 'final victory.'

As **Willard** says, '**Charlie** . . . had only two ways home, death or victory'. A conservative estimate would put North Vietnamese dead at around 750,000.

Vietnam War film

To some extent, any film made in Hollywood from the mid-1960s through the subsequent ten years was a **Vietnam War** film. Any filmmaker wanting to comment critically on America's involvement would have to tackle the subject obliquely. The conflict would be thinly disguised as World War II (as in *Kelly's Heroes*, which possibly supplied the idea of a musical accompaniment to a military attack, and *Catch-22*) or the Korean War (*M*A*S*H*). Hollywood's first official Vietnam War film was the John Wayne film *The Green Berets*, a piece of right-wing propaganda exposing the communist support for the **Viet Cong** and the dedication of the South Vietnamese army.

In the early to mid-1970s there were no mainstream Hollywood films about **Vietnam**. The coda to *American Graffiti* has Terry going missing in action in Vietnam and Kurt moving to Canada to become a writer, and presumably to avoid the draft. *Taxi Driver*'s Travis Bickle starts off slightly mad from his experiences in Vietnam. But it wasn't until the late 1970s, after the war, that Hollywood fully tackled the subject head on. The triple whammy of **Coming Home**, **The Deer Hunter** and *Apocalypse Now* explored the 'realities' of the war from, respectively, a left, right and ambivalent perspective. America, via Hollywood, was attempting to come to terms with the meaning of the war and the humiliating defeat. They achieved commercial success and official acceptance, announced through Oscars awarded, although the simpler, starker versions in *Coming Home* and *The Deer Hunter* were conspicuously more welcomed by the **Academy** than the more ambiguous *Apocalypse Now*. The huge Oscar success of *Platoon* served as America's declaration to the world that it had at last come to terms with the war.

Hollywood has, since *Apocalypse Now*, tackled the war comprehensively, if not always maturely or honestly. It is indicative of the lingering sense of national shame in defeat that a significant number of the films have presented a restaging of the war. This approach reached an entertaining but absurd nadir in Clint Eastwood's *Heartbreak Ridge*, in which America's recent military record in Korea and Vietnam is zero-one-one, i.e. won none, drawn one, lost one. Eastwood and his platoon of raw recruits rectify this situation with the glorious American victory in Grenada, thus making the record one-one-one.

John Rambo in *First Blood* is a representative of the vet returning from a war that the country wants to forget He is brilliant, resourceful and simply wants his country to love him as much as he loves it. In

Rambo: First Blood Part II he is returning to Vietnam to rescue American prisoners of war still held by the Vietnamese. He goes on the condition that 'This time we're allowed to win'. This plot structure was at the heart of a very short-lived sub-genre of the Vietnam film. *Uncommon Valor*, co-produced by **John Milius**, had the same basic plot. Apart from this, *Apocalypse Now* and *Big Wednesday*, Milius also tackled the American/communist conflict in a fanciful way in *Red Dawn*, in which resourceful American kids withstood a Soviet invasion of small-town America, and in *Flight of the Intruder*, a story of American naval pilots making a final attack on Hanoi.

There have been dozens of films that have dealt with Vietnam in one way or another, from melodramas and biopics to comedies, but none has been as authentic, fantastic or indeed funny as *Apocalypse Now*.

voice-over

The project had from the start been conceived of as accompanied by a voice-over narration. However, as **Walter Murch** explains:

> When I first got on the film the decision had been made not to use narration, even though it had been in the screenplay. **Francis [Coppola]** told me to drop the idea of narration, but when I actually started **editing** I couldn't see how it would work without the narration, because it had been shot as if there were narration. In addition to that we had to have the film done – we had to finish editing in a couple of months – and I didn't see any way to get around that problem without going back to narration. So, on my own initiative, I started recording the narration myself using my own voice and tried to structure it and to sell it. I had just come off *Julia* which was a narrated film so I was used to the device, it sounded normal to me. So I started putting the voice-over back into the project and people thought, 'Let's go with this.' Then **Michael Herr** was brought in to actually write

the narration and what he came up with was better than what we
had in the script originally.

The film is almost unimaginable without its voice-over, which provides so much of the character and mood, and also supplies many of
the best lines. It is an essential device, along with the dossier material,
also conceived by Murch, for linking the episodes together, making
sense of them, pushing the story ahead, commenting on the action
and beefing up the character of **Willard**. He would be a virtual cypher
without it, taciturn, with unspecified motivations, heartless, psychotic
and almost uninteresting. Herr's writing lends it the authenticity of a
real witness to the war. The use of a narrator enhances the film's links to
its chief literary source by imitating the structure of *Heart of Darkness*.
The time in which the narration occurs relative to the action shifts
from the present – **'Saigon! Shit!'**, **'Some day this war's gonna
end'** and **'Never get out of the boat'** are Willard's thoughts at the
time – to an unspecified time after the events, for example: 'Everyone
gets what they want. I wanted a mission and, for my sins, that's what
I got. They brought it up to me like room service. A real choice
mission and when it was over I'd never want another.' In this way
Willard stands in for both **Marlow** and the unnamed narrator. The
voice-over also frequently echoes **Conrad** in specific language (e.g.
'for my sins'), tone and use of repetition.

W

Walküre, die

Opera in three acts by Richard Wagner first performed in Munich in 1870. *Die Walküre* includes **'The Ride of the Valkyries'**, which accompanies the **Air Cavalry**'s dawn **helicopter** raid on the **Viet Cong** village.

See **'Ride of the Valkyries, The'**.

water burial

Chief Phillips has just been killed. In a hauntingly beautiful, slightly over-exposed scene, while **Willard** explains the mission to the wired and very upset **Chef**, **Lance** ritually daubs paint on **Chief**'s face. He lowers himself and Chief's body into the river, cradles his head, pushes him gently away, and after a few seconds the body disappears beneath the surface with barely a ripple.

In **Heart of Darkness**, after **Marlow** has pulled the spear out of the helmsman's side, he recalls that:

> His heels leaped together over the little door-step; his shoulders were pressed to my breast; I hugged him from behind desperately. Oh! He was heavy, heavy; heavier than any man on earth, I should imagine. Then without more ado I tipped him overboard. The current snatched him as though he had been a

wisp of grass and I saw the body roll over twice before I lost sight of it for ever.

water–skiing

The scene when **Willard** has just joined the crew of the **PBR** is one of the film's many instances of the importing of American style, customs and culture into **Vietnam**. It must have been inspired by Philip Jones Griffiths's photograph, which appears in his book *Vietnam Inc.* This layered image has in the background a line of palm trees, then the river bank dotted with shacks. On the river is a young man of indeterminate race, in silhouette, water-skiing towards the camera and apparently straight into a group of Vietnamese people working on their river boats in the foreground. Right at the front, out of focus, an elderly Vietnamese man in a broken hat stares straight at the camera.

This whole scene is recreated in the film. **Lance**, like the water–skier in the photo, is passing through these people's lives, indulging in a frivolous pastime, and recklessly, deliberately interfering with the serious day-to-day work of the people.

weapons

Walter Murch recalls his problems in recreating the authentic **sound** of the weapons seen and heard in the film:

The problem with the weaponry was simply that there wasn't anything recorded in stereo, as stereo was relatively new. The sound recordings of guns that were in the libraries were not in stereo and anyway they were mostly World War II and Korean War in vintage. We wanted to have the sound of guns and weaponry that accurately reflected the sound which soldiers had heard in **Vietnam**. So we had a whole recording session of live ammunition – AK47s and M16 rocket launchers, all that kind of stuff. It went on for a couple of days where we developed our own library in stereo using five or six recorders simultaneously.

Weston, Jessie L. (1850–1928)

Author writing mainly about the Arthurian legends. Her study *From Ritual to Romance*, which examines the Christian and pagan roots of the story of the Grail, is seen on the reading table in **Kurtz's library**.

White, Dick

One of the team of military advisers working on the film. He acted as the co-ordinator of jets and **helicopters** and served as **Coppola**'s personal pilot.

Wilder, Billy (b. 1906)

Great writer/director born in Sucha. He moved to Berlin as a young man and then, fleeing the Nazis, moved to France in 1933 and on to the USA the following year. In Hollywood he shared accommodation with Peter Lorre, and in 1938 began his screenwriting collaboration with Charles Brackett. Among their writing credits are *Ninotchka* and *Ball of Fire*. Their writing partnership survived Wilder's move into directing and continued until *Sunset Boulevard*. His films include *The Lost Weekend*, *Ace in the Hole*, *Stalag 17* and *Some Like It Hot*.

In early versions of the film there was an interval directly after the **sampan** massacre. At an invitation screening to the film Steven Bach, who had recently joined **United Artists** as a senior vice-president, was seated next to Wilder. When the interval came, Bach introduced himself to his idol, saying, 'Hi, I just wanted to say that I'm a big fan of yours. *Double Indemnity* and *Sunset Boulevard*, I particularly love.' Wilder interrupted him brusquely, saying, 'How can you mention those pieces of shit in the presence of this work of genius.'

Willard, Captain Benjamin L.

The surname conveniently suggests the idea of a resolute will, which instantly establishes a link between him and **Kurtz**. Kurtz has adopted the attitude that he has seen and so admires in the **Viet Cong**, the genius of their pure, crystalline will. It has been claimed that his two names were jokily chosen after **Harrison Ford**'s children. **Walter Murch** suggests:

> At the time *Apocalypse Now* was being written, there were two killer rat movies, *Willard* and its sequel *Ben*, and I think **John Milius** had something to do with those movies, so you get Benjamin Willard.

John Milius, however, denies this link and any connection to the 'rat movies'. Willard, like **Marlow** in *Heart of Darkness*, is the story's narrator, its eyes, and so is present in every scene. The film's story is Willard's journey. He is an **assassin**, a man of action, but is required – apart from **the beginning**, **end** and his sudden shooting of the **woman** on the **sampan** – to remain immobile, impassive and almost silent throughout the film's journey. Early on, when he is studying the dossier, he finds it impossible to reconcile the man emerging from the documents he is studying with the voice he heard in **Nha Trang**. In the same way, it is almost impossible to see the taciturn man on screen as the same man narrating the film. These two parts of Willard were written by different men, and reflect the change that Willard goes through on his quest.

Willard from the start is a nearly broken man, who, like Kurtz, has an intense empathy and admiration for the single-mindedness of his enemy. Also, like Kurtz and **Kilgore**, he is manifestly incapable of functioning outside the war. Both Willard and Kurtz are unable to communicate with their wives. Willard is incomplete, drawn by some mystical powers of Kurtz up the river, through a vision of the

Vietnam War, through the gates of hell into the heart of darkness. He has been summoned there by destiny working through the powers of Christian and pagan traditions involving vegetation rituals either summoned up by or controlling Kurtz. Arriving there, his own destiny is revealed to him, he fulfils his duty, slaughters the king, assumes his place as king, causes regeneration and then moves off into the heart of an immense darkness.

Whether you are convinced by the film's mystical conclusion – and I don't think you can or should be every time – it is a fascinating and beautifully conceived journey and film.

Wizard of Oz, The

Whether or not *The Wizard of Oz* was a conscious reference point for the film-makers, there are certain parallels between the two films. *Apocalypse Now* strives to place itself in an artistic, literary and mythical lineage. If you were forced at gunpoint to name the three key works of American art, cases could be made for *Huckleberry Finn*, *Moby Dick* and *The Wizard of Oz*. In the case of *Huckleberry Finn* there are no obvious borrowings or similarities other than that both are picaresque river journeys. Again, *Moby Dick* shares nothing with *Apocalypse Now* other than coincidentally telling the story of a boat travelling inexorably towards a fateful confrontation with a bloated, smooth-skinned nemesis. Brilliant!

The Wizard of Oz, though. The way the **Montagnards** re-emerge from their hiding places having been scared off by the sirens is very like the way the Munchkins come out when the Good Witch Glinda tells them to after Dorothy has landed on and killed the Wicked Witch of the East, sister of the more famous Wicked Witch of the West. Both films **end** with the central characters being revered by a newly liberated people whose evil, mad oppressor they have killed. Both films centre on a character plucked from the American Midwest and sent to a strange distant land. If the film-makers had stuck more closely to

Heart of Darkness in the aftermath of **Chef**'s killing, both would have sported red footwear. Both are told that they must take a long journey along one simple route, which they undertake with a few companions. They travel through forests with **puppies** and **tigers** and nearly bare **women**, and they come across poppies (in the excised opium-smoking scene, part of the **French plantation** sequence), before the route leads directly into the vast complex that houses the object of their quest. They are greeted at first by hostility, then by an eccentric man who ushers them into a world where normal rules no longer apply. The man whom they have been imagining all along the journey has been turned into a great and powerful god by his adopted people. But when they finally do confront him he turns out to be a plump bald man also from the Midwest of America. Both fulfil their destiny accompanied by a repeated phrase, and leave the place unsure (as is the audience) whether the man they encountered was great or just a fat old fake.

women

Women do not fare too well in the film. There are **Willard**'s and **Kurtz**'s estranged wives, the **Viet Cong** woman who blows up the **helicopter** and is pursued and shot, the **Playboy Bunnies**, the woman on the **sampan** killed by Willard, and the woman around Kurtz's compound, a version of Kurtz's native companion in *Heart of Darkness*. This matches the mood of **Conrad**'s novella. There you have **Marlow**'s aunt, the two women – one fat one thin – at the office when he gets his commission and Kurtz's fiancée, to whom Marlow **lies** at **the end**. As Marlow says, having been silent for a long time:

> 'I laid the ghost of his gifts with a lie', he began suddenly. 'Girl! What? Did I mention a girl? Oh, she is out of it – completely. They – the women I mean – are out of it – should be out of it. We must help them stay in that beautiful world of their own lest ours gets any worse.'

Wood, Cyndi

Playmate of the Year for 1974, who plays the Playmate of the Year Terri Foster. The quick wipe of the nose at the end of her walk to the front of the stage presumably suggests the character's cocaine use, another excample of the film's **drugs** theme.

In Peter Cowie's *Coppola* production designer **Dean Tavoularis** recalls a time when the typhoon struck the location:

> I was trapped for days in a house with the 'Playmate of the Year', who had been flown out to appear in the show sequence. She didn't want to live in a hotel, so I took her to this little basement room, and told her there was just the one room because three or four of us were already crammed into the place. We sat around and it started raining harder and harder until finally it was literally *white* outside, and all the trees were bent at forty-five degree angles. A writer from the *New York Times* happened to be trapped there with us, along with my brother, my nephew, my driver, and a toothless old man who lived permanently in the house. The writer, Jonathan Reynolds, later wrote a play, *Geniuses*, about a kind of chauvinistic art director trapped with a Playmate!

See **Playboy Bunnies**.

X

X-rays

See **death cards**.

Z

'Zap 'em with your sirens, man'

See **photo-journalist, the**.

Ziesmer, Jerry

Assistant director on the film, as well as playing Jerry, the civilian, whose only line on screen is one of the film's most famous.

See **'terminate with extreme prejudice'**.

Zoetrope

In 1969 **Coppola** began to realise his dream of establishing his own company. The company he formed in San Francisco with **George Lucas** and Mona Skager was called American Zoetrope. Zoetrope is derived from the ancient Greek word meaning 'life turn' and was the name given to a proto-cinematic device of the mid-nineteenth century. In this mechanism, sequential pictures were attached around the interior of its perforated barrel structure, which when viewed while being spun would convey the impression of a moving image. In *Notes*, **Eleanor** Coppola's diary entry for 26 August includes this apocalyptic insight:

He [Francis Coppola] has always wanted to be part of where it really was happening. He has always wanted to be in this wonderful community of artists at the moment that people would talk about later as some golden era. He tried to make it happen in San Francisco. He dreamed of this group of poets, film-makers and writers who would drink espresso in North Beach and talk of their work, and it would be good. They would publish their writing in *City* magazine, do new plays at the Little Fox Theatre, make experimental films at American Zoetrope. There would be this terrific center of exciting art. He spent a lot of money and energy trying to make it happen. When it didn't, he got angry and frustrated and maybe, mostly sad. He threw his Oscars out the window and left for **the Philippines**.

Well, just this morning, I realized that this is *it*! Right here in Pagsanjan [the location of **Kurtz**'s **temple** compound], of all places. I couldn't see it because it isn't some North Beach café or picturesque studio in Paris or a New York City loft. It's right here [in our own back yard – back to *The Wizard of Oz*]. Here we both are, right here where we dreamed of being. I started to laugh. When you stop looking for something, you see it right in front of you. This is the community of artists. It's **Dean [Tavoularis]**, Bob **[Duvall]**, **Vittorio [Storaro]**, Enrico [Umetelli], **Joe [Lombardi]**, Marty **[Sheen]** and Alfredo **[Marchetti]**. When I think about it, I really believe that this film is the most pertinent artwork going on today. We call what

Dean's doing, sets; that's an old label. He is probably making the most interesting art sculpture event going on anywhere in the world right now. Vittorio is a world-class visual artist. A poet with light. Francis is writing, only he is not in a romantic-looking garret, he is bent over his electric type-writer right here, sweating in Pagsanjan, so he doesn't see it. Francis is actually the conceptual artist I have been wanting to know. The most right-on artist of 1976. This is that moment we've dreamed of being present at. We're swatting mosquitoes, and eating mangos, it doesn't look like it's supposed to, but I'll bet this is that point in time somebody will label as *it*. I am still laughing.

This is a wonderful, poignant image that almost captures the whole appeal of the film for some people. Zoetrope as a name persists to this day; the company itself is much altered, having gone bankrupt along with the brilliant folly of *One From the Heart*. But this is a powerful idea – of some evanescent, perfect, crystalline moment when, by chance and design, Coppola's dream came true, possibly without him realising it, in the creation of a work of art that would capture and hold an audience for at least twenty years. This film became inadvertently the realisation of Coppola's hopes for Zoetrope. He found himself in the midst of, at the centre of, a film production that was so logistically complex and time-consuming that it became a significant creative phase, almost constituting a movement.

The result of this effort is a film that retains its power to dazzle and move, and which in its conception arguably cost Coppola much of his creative drive. The process did not change just the director, as **John Milius** says:

Everybody who had anything to do with that film was affected in some way – much the way that **Vietnam** vets were affected – it was like there was some powerful medicine, 'big medicine' like the Indians say. It was about the war, it was as if the war had infected the film, the tragedy of the war, the human size of the war. It was like we were making the film and people who had nothing to do with the war were suddenly in the middle of it. It was as if the war were somehow sacred.'

'The horror! The horror!'

Bibliography

Adair, Gilbert, *Hollywood's Vietnam*, Heinemann, 1989

Auster, Albert and Quart, Leonard, *How the War was Remembered: Hollywood and Vietnam*, Praeger, 1988

Bach, Steven, *Final Cut*, Pimlico, 1996

Beauchamp, Carri and Béhar, Henri, *Hollywood on the Riviera: The Inside Story of the Cannes Film Festival*, William Morrow, 1992

Blinn, James, *The Aardvark is Ready for War*, Doubleday, 1997

Boorman, John and Donohue, Walter, *Projections 6*, Faber & Faber, 1996

Brady, Frank, *Citizen Welles*, Hodder & Stoughton, 1989

Braestrup, Peter, *Big Story*, Anchor, 1978

Brando, Marlon, with Lindsey, Robert, *Songs My Mother Taught Me*, Century, 1994

Bugliosi, Vincent, *Helter Skelter*, W. W. Norton, 1974

Callow, Simon, *Orson Welles: The Road to Xanadu*, Jonathan Cape, 1995

Conrad, Joseph, *Congo Diary and Other Uncollected Pieces*, edited by Zdizlaw Najder, Doubleday, 1978

Conrad, Joseph, *Heart of Darkness*, Penguin, 1983

Conrad, Joseph, *Heart of Darkness* (critical edition), edited by Robert Kimbrough, Norton, 1988

Coppola, Eleanor, *Notes: On the Making of Apocalypse Now*, Faber & Faber, 1995

Cowie, Peter, *Coppola*, Faber & Faber, 1990

Dagens, Bruno, *Angkor: Heart of an Ancient Empire*, Thames & Hudson, 1989

Eliot, T. S., *Selected Poems*, Faber & Faber, 1954

Fenton, James, *Granta 15: The Fall of Saigon*, Granta, 1985

Frazer, James George, *The Golden Bough*, Oxford University Press, 1994

Goethe, Johann Wolfgang von, *Faust*, Penguin, 1949

Grobel, Lawrence, *Conversations with Marlon Brando*, Bloomsbury, 1991

Hargrove, Jim, *Martin Sheen: Actor and Activist*, Children's Press, 1991

Hendrickson, Paul, *The Living and the Dead: Robert McNamara and Five Lives of a Lost War*, Macmillan, 1997

Herr, Michael, *Dispatches*, Picador, 1978

Holden, Anthony, *The Oscars*, Warner, 1994

Houseman, John, *Unfinished Business*, Columbus Books, 1986

Jones, John R., *Guide to Vietnam*, Bradt, 1989

Jones Griffiths, Philip, *Vietnam Inc.*, Collier, 1971

Karnow, Stanley, *Vietnam: A History*, Guild, 1983

Lewis, Jon, *Whom God Wishes to Destroy: Francis Coppola and the New Hollywood*, Athlone, 1995

McCarthy, Mary, *Medina*, Wildwood House, 1973

Manso, Peter, *Brando*, Weidenfeld & Nicolson, 1994

Mico, Ted, Miller-Monzon, John and Rubel, David (eds) *Past Imperfect: History According to the Movies*, Henry Holt, 1995

Miller, Russell, *Magnum*, Secker & Warburg, 1997

Page, Tim, *Page After Page*, Paladin, 1990

Pollock, Dale, *Skywalking: The Life and Films of George Lucas*, Elmtree Books, 1983

Pye, Michael and Myles, Linda, *The Movie Brats*, Faber & Faber, 1979

Said, Lawrence H., *Guts & Glory: Great American War Movies*, Addison Wesley, 1978

Salt, Barry, *Film Style & Technology: History and Analysis*, Starword, 1992

Schell, Jonathan, *The Real War*, Corgi, 1989

Schickel, Richard, *Brando: A Life in Our Times*, Pavilion, 1991

Schurmann, Franz, Dale Scott, Peter and Zelnik, Reginald, *The Politics of Escalation in Vietnam*, Fawcett, 1966

Sheehan, Neil, *A Bright Shining Lie*, Jonathan Cape, 1989

Smith, Julian, *Looking Away: Hollywood and Vietnam*, Scribner, 1975

Southam, B. C., *A Student's Guide to the Selected Poems of T. S. Eliot*, Faber & Faber, 1968

Tomalin, Nicholas, *Nicholas Tomalin Reporting*, André Deutsch, 1975

Virgil, *The Aeneid of Virgil*, translated by Allen Mandelbaum, Bantam, 1981

Weston, Jessie L., *From Ritual to Romance*, Princeton University Press, 1993

Wintle, Justin, *The Vietnam Wars*, Weidenfeld & Nicolson, 1991

Wolfe, Tom, *The New Journalism*, with an anthology edited by Tom Wolfe and E. W. Johnson, Picador, 1975

Wood, Robin, *Hollywood from Vietnam to Reagan*, Columbia University Press, 1986

Acknowledgements

Thanks to Fiona, my family and friends for help and encouragement, in particular my parents, and Sean and Nicci for reading through the manuscript. Special gratitude to Steven Bach, Richard Marks, John Milius and Walter Murch for generously sparing the time to speak to me about their experiences working on the film. Equally I want to thank my godfather Col. (retired) William Hokanson for responding to my various enquiries about his tours of duty in Vietnam, and Phil Beynon for his invaluable historical knowledge. Thanks to the BFI library and information service, and the Cinema Store, St. Martin's Lane. Grateful thanks to the following for useful pointers, advice, information and the loan of books, tapes etc.: Robin Holt, Joe Laniado, David Parkinson, Zak Reddan, Marc Vaulbert. Finally thanks to everyone at Bloomsbury especially Michael Jones and Will Webb, and most of all Matthew Hamilton who initiated the project and patiently tolerated my repeated assurances that 'One day this book's gonna end.'